The essential introduction to home-based education

FOURTH EDITION

education otherwise

Education Otherwise
PO Box 7420, London N9 9SG

First published 1981
Second edition 1985
Third edition 1993

Fourth edition 1996

ISBN 0 9521703 1 0

Foreword

Nothing stays the same for long. Even as the last edition of *School is not compulsory* went to press, the Education Act 1993 was going through Parliament. As a result the booklet was out of date almost as soon as it was published. Admittedly the 1993 Act contained little that was new with respect to home education, but it did restate many existing provisions. This meant the Education Act 1944 could no longer be accurately described as 'the main piece of legislation relating to education in England and Wales'.

This edition includes references to the new Act. It also incorporates a much more significant change for England and Wales, namely the Education (Pupil Registration) Regulations 1995 (see page 51). And in addition it contains a much more careful and systematic treatment of Scottish law (sections 2.6 and 2.8). Unfortunately it hasn't been practicable to deal with Northern Irish law in the same way. The law in Northern Ireland is basically the same as in England, but you would be well advised to check locally before attempting to cite it. (The law in the Republic of Ireland is summarised in section 2.10. This section is based on material provided by Clare Weber.)

It seems a long time now since the first, 26-page edition of *School is not compulsory* was published in 1981. It was written by Dick Kitto, who also played a leading part in founding Education Otherwise. Since then the publication has grown like a snowball, as with each edition successive layers have been added to the original core. In 1985, Bruce and Dianne Cox gave it its present three-part structure, revising the original material and adding extensive accounts of personal experience written by home educating parents. In 1993 we in turn reworked the material and added a number of new sections, including one on special educational needs contributed by Sylvia Jeffs.

In the foreword to the last edition we wrote, 'Inevitably this edition in turn will soon be out of date'. With this fourth edition we need to say the same thing again, but we hope our prediction won't come true quite as rapidly as it did on the last occasion.

As time goes on it becomes increasingly difficult to name everyone who has contributed to the evolution of *School is not compulsory* with material, comments or both. But we should like to thank them all, including the authors of the many quotations which form such an important element of the booklet. And finally, thanks to Sarah Guthrie and Sarah Lawrence for the illustrations.

Anne Wade
Rob Wade

Abbreviations

In this booklet, the expression *the 1944 Act* means the Education Act 1944. *The 1993 Act* means the Education Act 1993. *The Scottish Act* means the Education (Scotland) Act 1980.

LEA stands for 'local education authority'. Strictly speaking this expression applies to England and Wales only, but we have often used it loosely for any local government authority dealing with education. We apologise for this to readers elsewhere in the UK. *DFEE* means 'Department for Education and Employment' (previously the Department for Education, and before that the Department of Education and Science), the government department responsible for education in England.

EO usually stands for Education Otherwise Association; but in quotations it is sometimes used to mean home-based education in general.

Comments

If you have noticed any omissions or inaccuracies, or if you would like to make suggestions of any kind, we would be glad to hear from you. Please write to Anne and Rob Wade care of the address on the back of the title page; or see the Education Otherwise contact list under West London.

CONTENTS

3 Your relationship with the local education authority

Appendices

at an EO Christmas party Mrs G meets a teacher ...
and you teach 20 children all by yourself? How do you have the PATIENCE?
& don't you worry about them mixing only with their peer group?
What about when they're older & have to sit exams?
and supposing we ALL kept our children in school?
don't get me wrong — I'm just fascinated, that's all
I couldn't do it, I must say, but I take my hat off to you
CRISP?
SLUMP
EDUCATING ARCHIE at Christmas
by SEG

Introduction

Education is legally compulsory - schooling is not

> It shall be the duty of the parent of every child of compulsory school age to cause him to receive efficient full-time education suitable to his age, ability, and aptitude, and to any special educational needs he may have, either by regular attendance at school **or otherwise**.
>
> *Education Act 1944, section 36*
> *(as amended by the Education Act 1981, section 17), emphasis added.*

In Britain, as in all developed countries, nearly all children go to school. But they don't have to. The law says parents must see that their children are properly educated, but it leaves them the choice of how to do it.

If you are thinking of educating your child outside the school system, this booklet is for you. It doesn't aim to show you in detail *how* to educate your child, but it does try to answer a number of basic questions. In particular it outlines the legal basis of out-of-school education and discusses some practical issues which are likely to arise in your relationship with the authorities. But above all it contains a variety of personal experience in the words of parents and children who have already embarked on home-based education.

You may find the legal part of this booklet rather forbidding. Most laws are concerned with what you can't do, not what you can. They seem to deal with penalties more than rights. But the law can also be seen as a protection against the arbitrary exercise of authority. And although only a tiny number of home educators are ever involved in legal action, you will need to be clear about your rights and duties if you are to communicate with the authorities effectively.

Of all those parents who practise home-based education, the vast majority do so without encountering serious difficulties, usually with the full cooperation of the authorities. To achieve this end, it's important to begin on the right footing. We hope this booklet helps.

Institutions may be created for the best of reasons, but we can become entrapped in them. Our job as responsible citizens is to monitor them constantly, to help them serve us and live up to their best aims, and not to allow them to dominate us. We need to know how they work in order to work with them and also at times to work against them. We cannot do everything, but we can become well equipped to negotiate one or two areas of bureaucracy, and we can empower each other by sharing this information and skill when someone else needs it.

This is what this booklet is for.

1

Learning at home

1.1 Reasons

Why do parents choose to educate their children out of school?

- They may feel that schools are failing their children and they can learn more effectively at home.
- They may want their children to be exposed to more positive values than those prevalent in schools.
- They may feel that schools as a social institution cannot provide the sort of education they would like for their children.
- They may wish to provide a specific religious environment for their children.
- They may want to prevent schools from harming their children.
- There may be problems with bullying or school refusal.

Some parents choose not to send their children to school on principle:

> ▸ I saw no reason why I should hand over the responsibility for my children's education to somebody else when I had managed quite happily for the previous five years.

Sometimes there is no question about this from the start, but in many cases there is an ambivalence which continues until the child reaches 'school age':

> ▸ Initially the question was academic, but as time passed we realised we would have to make a decision - dare we stand out against the system or would we sink our growing convictions and fall into line with

everyone else we knew and send ours to school at the magic age of five?

Some foresee that their children's interests will be better served by home-based education:

▸ The reason I joined EO was because I noticed the way Paul learned things up to the age of five, and I became increasingly concerned that this easy, uncomplicated way of learning would have to stop when he went to school.

▸ We gradually became involved in home education by just watching our son develop and through the realisation that school would have nothing positive to offer him, but would indeed strip him of his confidence and self-motivation.

▸ Having seen the rapid and joyful development of our child we are extremely concerned that entry into either state or private education will place her in a mental and emotional straitjacket, squashing her fiery nature and enquiring mind.

Who can educate their children out of school?

Contrary to popular opinion, you don't have to be a teacher to educate children at home. Nor do you have to have had any higher education yourself. Home educators come from all walks of life. Qualifications may give confidence, but all you really need is a desire to help your children learn and the motivation to make home education work.

Some parents expect to take responsibility for their children's education for an indefinite period; others simply feel that at the age of five their children are still too young to go to school:

▸ Another major reason for educating at home was that we considered that Anne would not be ready to leave home at five years old. She needed more self-assurance before this would be the case. We preferred the system of other European countries whose children remain at home until seven.

▸ Even our visiting adviser said that she couldn't understand why more parents didn't consider not sending their children to school at five; she thought it was far too young.

Sometimes their own memories of school are painful ones:

▸ How could I send her down the road on a path that I was still trying to recover from?

Such parents often seek reassurance that they are not working out their own problems through their children:

▸ Were we really interested in our children's growth and development or were we just working out, through them, unresolved aggravations and conflicts from our own childhood?

What does home education cost?

It's only as expensive as you choose to make it. Generally speaking direct expenditure is negligible in comparison with even the cheapest private education - and of course there are some financial savings in not sending a child to school. At worst, the main cost is loss of earnings and perhaps career prospects on the part of one parent. Most home educating families aren't rich, and many live on very low incomes.

For many parents it can become a practical necessity to withdraw their children from school when its effects on them become apparent:

▸ The first term had a disastrous effect on her character and personality.

▸ He became severely bad-tempered, frustrated and aggressive and every day arrived home with a list of complaints, in a state of depression and negativity.

▸ She used to be a child that tackled anything. Now she gives up and doesn't believe she can do it. When we think how confident and outgoing she used to be - we could cry.

▸ We felt quite desperate for an alternative to school after John and Paul's dismal failure within two senior schools.

Often there is a contrast between behaviour at home and at school:

> ▸ Bright, eager, interested at home, he somehow 'couldn't concentrate', 'couldn't remember' at school. He was always forgetting: not only the times tables and how to spell 'there', but also the note from school, the wellington boots...

Or else there may be a noticeable difference between one child who has been withdrawn and another who is still attending:

> ▸ While John has relaxed, matured and grown in confidence, Richard, still at school, has begun to show the same symptoms as John previously - aches and pains, fatigue, anxiety, tension, aggressiveness, self-doubt.

What if I'm a single parent?

Many single parents home educate successfully. If you work part-time you may be able to arrange for your child to be with you and get on with work in a quiet corner. Older children may be happy to be left alone for part of the day, or to spend the time with another home educating family. Sometimes cooperative arrangements may extend to communal living.

Sometimes stress originating at school can express itself in behaviour at home:

> ▸ At home he had severe temper tantrums and bouts of crying lasting for half an hour to two hours, although these never occurred at school. We told the school what was happening but they did not seem particularly concerned.

And sometimes the problem can be exacerbated by signs of school refusal (see page 38):

> ▸ He was becoming increasingly anxious, even panicky; had all kinds of aches and pains every morning and on the way to school; and although one of the 'top' readers, was reluctant to read, wept for fear of 'questions', and begged not to have to go to school.
>
> Leaving him at the gate every morning was a protracted business; but having the occasional quiet word with his teacher solved only a few isolated problems and did not improve the overall situation - nor his relationship with the teacher. At home he was tense, sulky, fearful;

> spoke in a 'school' idiom which owed more to television than to any authentic child subculture; was very quick to jeer or boast. At the same time he produced work at home far superior in liveliness and imagination to anything he did at school - and had to be taken away from all this in order to get ready for school every morning... It reminded me of the old joke about the nurse waking the patient to give him sleeping tablets.

My child has special educational needs. Can I educate him or her at home?

Yes. This is discussed in detail below (beginning on page 60).

Parents who have seen the way in which their child has been influenced by school may be incensed to find the child and home background blamed for his or her failure to 'fit in':

> ▸ The LEA inspector asked if I had thought of the school psychiatrist before removing Mark, so I put it to him, as gently as I could, that I wasn't puzzled by Mark's inability to adjust to a school that was so unresponsive to his needs.

Whether they choose from the beginning not to send their children to school, or whether they decide to withdraw them from school in response to a problem that has arisen there, all home educating parents have opted to take back responsibility for their children from the state. This decision is often not an easy one, but the benefits are frequently greater than expected...

1.2 Starting out

Few parents take up home-based education on impulse, even if the decision itself appears to be quite sudden. As one parent writes, 'My subconscious had been playing with the idea for years.' Once you have begun to consider the possibility, you may feel you need information and support. One way of getting them is to join Education Otherwise, read its publications, and meet as many practising members as possible (see page 123). Not only will this give you confidence and answer a host of questions; it will also provide your children with a chance to meet others who are out of school, so that they are less likely to feel odd or unusual.

In the end, though, each family is unique. When it comes to deciding whether to take the final plunge, you will be on your own, and this decision may take some courage:

> ▸ We visited several EO families further afield to gain first hand information. These meetings were invaluable boosts to our thinking and each time we came away convinced we could manage. But as time passed, so did our self-confidence. We realised that our biggest difficulty lay within us - our own fears of standing out against the accepted way of doing things, our fear of how the LEA would respond to our decision.

> ▸ I was contacted by someone whose child had been at school for a year and was in the same position as me - dithering on the verge. It's amazing what a difference it makes to have someone to sound out your doubts on. After that I found out about other EO families, practising or dithering. It took Matthew and myself a year and a term to take the plunge, and this is now our second term of EO.

But it may not take you long to realise you have made the right choice:

> ▸ We agonised over the decision to take her out, researching all the alternatives and talking it over with anyone who would listen. Then a friend said, 'I don't know why you are dithering. I don't see you have any option when she's in such a state.'
>
> Within days of telling her she need not go back, Laura's disturbed behaviour subsided, just as it had done each school holiday. We could only wonder what all our fuss had been about - it was all so straightforward and obviously right.
>
> It was a wasted, damaging time, that year in school. But she quickly went back to learning as she had done before - on her own terms, with great enthusiasm and energy, in a very individual way. Admittedly, few schools could have coped with it, but it was no problem in a home

situation. It's sheer delight to watch how a child's mind develops when you don't limit it, how the small child's integrity and clarity can be maintained and yet combined with a growing reasoning ability that is impressively powerful.

Once the decision is made, the practical steps towards home-based education will depend on your particular situation. If your child has only just reached the age of five, it may simply be a case of carrying on as before. If you are taking an older child out of school, you will normally need to explain your intentions to the authorities. (For England and Wales see pages 51 and 78; for Scotland see pages 59 and 81).

What will the authorities say?

LEAs vary a great deal in their attitudes to 'otherwise' education, but if you are well informed you are unlikely to be involved in serious conflict. Part 2 of this booklet explains your rights and duties, and part 3 discusses your relationship with the LEA in detail.

Adjustment may be difficult at first, and you may be glad of practical and emotional support:

▸ To begin with, my whole day was completely taken up with the new situation; I felt that I was undergoing a crash-course in teacher-training, I was trying to rethink all my assumptions about education, and at the same time I felt isolated and this made me feel unsure of myself. The turning point really was when the first batch of booklets, newsletters and so on came from EO - there is nothing like reading your own ideas clearly formulated by someone else, and supported by others, to give you strength in any enterprise! They also gave me practical details and facts to go on, so that I felt better grounded. I felt an enormous respect for those who managed to deschool their children before there was any support. I also read *Teach your own...*

As more and more families embark on home-based education, a fund of collective experience builds up, and the way becomes easier. Once you have become a confident and practised 'otherwise' educator, you will in turn be in a position to help, support and enable other families.

(For the origin of the expression 'education otherwise', see page 42.)

1.3 Rewards and benefits

The effect of withdrawing a child from school can sometimes take time to show itself:

▸ The first year out of school was a very difficult one. Andrew's confidence had been greatly undermined and his health was low. He felt he had failed and was afraid and embarrassed to meet any of his friends from school, as he was afraid of being teased for opting out, but he absolutely refused to go back to his old school or have anything to do with any other. Any suggestion which came from the LEA was immediately suspect by virtue of its source, regardless of its validity.

It seemed to us that he suddenly changed and began to become a 'social animal' again, but I'm sure this was only the outward appearance and that the healing process within himself had been a gradual one. I think two things took place:

- He discovered through chance meetings that in-school friends were extremely envious of his new freedom from school and, rather than wanting to taunt him, they thought it was a victory; and
- It took him some time to really believe that it mightn't all be a dream and any minute now he might be whisked back.

Finding we were solidly behind him (although suspected of not understanding because we were adults - another species?) did wonders for his morale.

But whether it takes a long time or not, the change is likely to be striking:

▸ The advantages and disadvantages of our new life are showing themselves already. Sandra is still struggling and emotional upheavals are still common (and very wearing I must confess) but at least we are beginning to find the skeletons in her cupboard, instead of refusing to admit they are there and hushing them up. David can now add up and subtract in HTU sums (including borrowings etc) and we have read ten books in our reading scheme. He loves them and is all the keener now that the writing is normal size and there are more than three words on a line!

▸ I think there would never have been a question of giving up what we were doing, because the change in James was so palpably an improvement. It was very moving, after a couple of weeks of home education, to hear him singing; he sat in the sandpit running sand through his fingers, and sang - I couldn't remember when he had last seemed happy, compared to this. It interests me that the Steiner teaching lays emphasis on the physical aspect in the early years, for James' relaxation has taken a physical form. Always rigidly tense, he had taken part gingerly if at all in school games and PE; now his whole body has begun to soften. He loves to go to adventure playgrounds, or to set up games in the garden; he leads the other two in games which involve a lot of dressing up, face and body painting; there is much freer posturing, gesturing and dramatics generally.

▸ When we did deschool them they were quite sad about leaving, but now seven months on they have no desire to return. Having seen the change in them in those seven months, we just couldn't send them back. It is the whole idea of school and its place as a social institution encompassing the damaging effects of peer pressure, loss of personal responsibility for the use of one's time, television viewing, different attitudes and examples causing confusion within the child, seven and a half hours a day out of the family setting and so on.

But not all home educators necessarily have a strongly rooted antipathy to schools. Indeed, there are families who have children both in school and out. Most of those who don't send their children to school tend not to consider themselves 'anti-school' but rather 'pro-home education'. They usually feel that their care and concern as parents provide a basis for an education of a better kind than that available at school:

▸ Since deciding to educate our child ourselves, we have been amazed at just how much she can absorb and understand, and the insatiable thirst she has for knowledge. We have been able to utilise this attitude and been able to sustain this healthy thirst, whereas at school she would have been left to her own devices and probably become bored and uninterested. We have been able to iron out any initial learning problems before the subject became incomprehensible to her. At home she can learn at her own pace and time, and play can be directed at any difficulties over learning which might arise. Learning for both child and parent becomes an adventure and mutual admiration abounds.

▸ We all need the freedom to develop and learn at our own pace - I can give that to my children at home. No-one else can see more clearly and with the interest so necessary the stages, phases, needs and abilities of my children. I can see how different they are emotionally now, how their creative imagination has developed, how rarely they fall out with each other and how closely knit they are as brothers and sister. They feel no need to compete with each other - or anyone else for that matter.

They are learning that it is up to them to get things done, learning to finish what they start and that regular practice results in growing ability.

▸ While the housekeeping has suffered a little, our creative output has increased tenfold! I do not now feel that there is any question at all of choice between school and home education, as far as our family is concerned. It is only a matter of finding out how to improve on what we have achieved already.

▸ In June 1981 Nick sat seven O-levels at our local technical college as an external examinee... The day of the results dawned, and not wishing to wait any longer than need be, Nick cycled to the college to collect his grades. To his delight, he found he had gained all grade A's, the top grade. He telephoned me immediately and I experienced one of the best moments of my life. Our success was all the sweeter because of the cynicism and scepticism endured for so long.

Now I feel the three-and-a-half years my son spent at home have benefitted all the family. We all see the results of the experiment which allowed him to study quietly at his own pace in his own way whilst not being subjected to the endless time-wasting practices of school.

Of course, home education can sometimes be hard work:

▸ The main temptation to abandon my poor children to the clutches of power-crazy teachers is not social pressure, or lack of faith in my ability to direct them, or concern for their isolation, but fatigue; pure tiredness. We all have stories of changing nappies, playing Snakes and Ladders, answering the phone, baking a cake and explaining the Theory of Papal Infallibility at the same time, and whilst it all somehow seems to get done, it leaves you utterly drained the next day.

Particularly if your children are young, you may find it difficult to create time which is your own. But this may be essential:

▸ I do believe it is wise for the teacher/parent to make sure that he/she gets time off from the daily routine in order to re-orientate as an adult, without feeling guilty about it, because a refreshed adult is more efficient and more fun.

Possible solutions are to have one day off a week in which the children are looked after by someone else; to arrange for children to stay with another family on a reciprocal basis; or to have social get-togethers with other home-educating families. It's usually difficult to moan to people who aren't involved in 'otherwise' education. Not only are they likely to be intellectually uncomprehending, but they may also feel emotionally threatened. This could make them unsympathetic and quick to suggest sending your children to school.

But for most people the rewards of home-based education outweigh the problems:

> ▸ Most frequently asked of us is, 'Isn't it hard and tiring on parents?' Unquestionably, it is mentally, emotionally and physically demanding but after six months of EO our earlier trepidation has proved groundless and we look forward to an exciting three years with two young sons again balanced, happy and eager now that they are no longer subjected to harassment and intimidation.

> ▸ The children have been educated at home for nine months and during that time I feel I have unlearned so much it almost hurts. But it is a healthy sort of strain, like exercising muscles that have been disused since childhood. I have had days of doubt about whether I can stand to have no peace and quiet ever again, and the odd whim to pursue a career of my own, but I know I will never be able to hand over the reins of my children's lives to another body unless it is at their request.

And the sheer freedom of home-based education serves to show more clearly that school itself can impose a multitude of stresses on the whole family:

> ▸ What a relief to be free from school-runs and their mornings of shouting, screaming and panic-stations. And it's nice too (and cheaper) to be rid of school uniform, endless runny noses, swear words, tantrums, overtiredness, bitching and general lack of opportunity to do our own thing (except in those crowded two hours between four and six p.m., when parents and children alike drive themselves to death trying to fit everything in). We get the swimming baths to ourselves, we can have piano or horse-riding

lessons during the day, we can go to the dentist or the doctor when it suits us, and we can do all those lovely follow-up field trips which help to bring our lessons alive. We can take a day off when we feel like it or need it, instead of having 6-8 long weeks together, when everyone gets sick of doing nothing much, and we can take our family holidays when we like and revel in the peace and quiet and the cheaper rates.

In short, parents often find that home education adds an immensely valuable and enjoyable dimension to their family lives:

▸ The main advantage is happy children. And, for myself, a new delight in learning along with the children.

▸ Their time, and our time as a family, is our own again - our lives belong to us.

▸ Apart from the beneficial effects on the boys' personalities and on our family relationships, the main advantage of EO for us as a way of life has been the astonishingly liberating sense of not being bound by externally imposed restrictions on hours, dates, place, clothing and the rest. With this liberation has come a release of creative energy, a host of new ideas, a new interest in life for all of us. Instead of feeling hampered from leading any life of my own, I have begun to take up my old interests again - and that in itself stimulates their activities too.

I am still amazed at my good fortune in making this particular decision. It *has* 'made all the difference'.

▸ I think it has been the best part of my life so far and want it to continue for us both.

But perhaps the last word should be left to a home educated student:

▸ Overall I can say that being deschooled was a turning point in my life - a transformation from misery to contentment and confidence.

1.4 Methods

There are as many styles of home education as there are families doing it. Indeed, within any family, given the opportunity, each child (or adult) will develop and learn in their own particular way. Some parents may value a formal, structured approach, possibly to the extent of a fixed timetable and maybe even 'school' holidays. To others this would be anathema - their choice may be for an entirely child-led approach, believing that to attempt to 'teach' something which is of no interest to the child is not only a pointless and time-consuming exercise but also contributes to the dulling of the child's natural curiosity:

> ▸ I try not to become over-anxious about having 'something to show' as a result of their interest in a subject. If nurtured appropriately the interest will grow. If I try to guide the interest in the direction I think it should go, the child feels it is no longer his/her idea, they are no longer in control and they start to switch off mentally and the learning stops.

If the child has never been to school, the age of five may hold little significance: frequently a style of learning develops naturally from what has gone before. But in any case the transition to home education is relatively easy for younger children. They are less liable to be damaged and 'turned off', and will often spontaneously and joyously get on with learning what they need. Home education is likely to get easier with every year, as they become more independent and intent on what they want to learn.

But taking an older child out can sometimes be a more difficult transition. For many families in this situation, 'otherwise' education is not a premeditated act based on some prior conviction, but a response to some crisis or long-drawn-out failure in their children's schooling. The child may have developed an aversion to any form of conventional study. They may be very hurt and angry from years of misery, and relations may be strained after constant battling to get them to school.

The dramatic step of taking a child out can often mend the rift - you've proved you do care; you've listened at last and found the solution. But they may need a very long fallow period in which to recover and regain confidence, an emotional convalescence to mend the years of pain. In these circumstances parents may have to wait for some time before intellectual progress can become a priority. At the same time they may be faced with the often difficult task of justifying their arrangements to the LEA (see page 85).

Inevitably they will feel insecure and anxious at first. They could well be tempted to over-reach themselves and impose too much structure in an attempt to mimic some of the features of school education. Their insistent pressure may be more harmful than the more impersonal pressures of school. Whilst the child may need some kind of guidance over the day's activities, emotional stability is more important than formal education, and it may be wise not to insist on too much.

Will we have to follow the national curriculum?

No. See page 92 below.

Many families make several false starts and go through considerable experimentation before they settle down into a workable routine:

> ▸ We experimented doggedly with different 'timetables' and 'schemes', all of which ended up in the waste paper bin. We tried alternate days (mornings only) but found that Dominic could not keep occupied on his 'day off' without constantly interrupting what his sister was trying to do. We tried using schools programmes (some of which are very good but too short) but got ourselves into such a muddle trying to incorporate them into our day on a regular basis that Mum nearly had a brainstorm and no-one could go out or finish what they were doing because such and such a programme was about to start. So we abandoned TV except for one or two favourites (mostly afternoon programmes which we watch if and when we have finished our more interesting and challenging things).
>
> So we ended up doing some formal work each morning, early, on the basis of one hour on and one hour off for each child. In the intervening hour the child who is 'off' works unsupervised on routine consolidation of what has been learned already. New work of course is done with me, plus any problems that have cropped up.

But whatever position they set out from, families almost inevitably find their education becoming less formal as they gain confidence and find schoolroom methods less and less relevant. Home-based education offers real advantages in the flexibility and opportunity for creativity it affords. Moreover, the teacher-learner distinction is rarely as clear-cut as it is at

EDUCATING ARCHIE
BY SEG
the woman's mad
No structure? Really? How brave...
thank god we got Miranda into Rhodeales
—and you don't bother about games? No - absolutely..
crazed dangerous mish-mash
—no timetable? no worry about exams? Super.
but what do you do about textbooks?
oh we let the school borrow them occasionally

school, and out-of-school education is often a learning experience for the whole family:

> ▸ Our timetable is not rigid; enthusiasm is encouraged in any area of learning or interest and we continually seek to extend our awareness and knowledge. Whereas we had initially tended to clockwatch and were anxious if we found we had diverted from World Geography to Current Affairs and Politics or from Angles and Tangents to Aerial Navigation, we now are excited by our children's inquisitive minds and ability to encompass a vast range of topics. I frequently find difficulty in tearing myself away from a subject which I earlier had scant knowledge of and am discovering afresh with them.

In this booklet we often describe education otherwise than at school as 'home education'. But this is just a shorthand, and 'otherwise' education rarely takes place exclusively in the home. Out-of-school education that is simply home education is likely to get claustrophobic, particularly as children grow older. The real choice is not between school and home, but rather between school and the world beyond. Perhaps it would be less misleading to talk about 'home-*based* education' or 'out-of-school education', or even 'real world education'.

What facilities will we need?

Even conventional textbook courses may assume the use of a surprisingly modest range of resources, many of which can be improvised. It's quite possible to take GCSE physics, chemistry and biology by correspondence course without requiring laboratory facilities. With diminishing expenditure, schools themselves are often very short of equipment. Although the contents of a science laboratory or computer room may seem impressive, access to this equipment by children may be so limited and tightly controlled as to render it of questionable value. Home educating families are likely to have access to libraries, sports centres, TV, radio, computers and countless other resources, but what the home educated child can be most rich in is the time and attention of adults, when and where it's needed.

'Otherwise' children may have to forego the facilities of the school, but they may be able to gain access to resources in the outside world which are simply not available to school children. Instead of being artificially confined to classrooms, they may have the chance to see how people spend their working lives. This could extend to direct 'hands on' experience, perhaps through acting as 'apprentices' in various fields of adult activity. Of course, this is not to condone economic exploitation, and any such arrangements would clearly have to be educationally motivated.

Work experience

Legally, children can have work experience as part of their last year of compulsory education, but the arrangements have to be made or approved by the LEA as part of an educational programme. One Jehovah's Witness being educated at school did pioneering (full time ministry) and wrote it up as an official project; but more typically it could mean working two afternoons a week in a garage, or spending a fortnight working in an old people's home.

In one case a boy at school was truanting and working full time for a greengrocer. The LEA prosecuted his parents and the greengrocer, and the boy returned to school. He was then put on full time, five days a week, work experience - with a greengrocer.

If your child is being educated at home and wants to work, you may find you can arrange something with your LEA's cooperation. Normally speaking it would be hard to present an extended period of full time work as part of your provision. But one family had a fifteen year old boy who was interested in nothing but car maintenance. They proposed a programme of home education based mainly on working in a garage, which the LEA accepted.

The relevant law is the Education (Work Experience) Act 1973. It applies to England, Wales and Scotland, but not to Northern Ireland.

Taking your children out of school doesn't necessarily mean doing it all yourself. In the first place, other children are often excellent tutors for younger ones. But you may also find people in your locality who can be involved. If there are other home educating families nearby with a similar outlook, you may be able to work cooperatively with them, sharing skills and perhaps clubbing together to hire tutors for areas of study which you can't cover for yourselves. Tutors often advertise their services in local newspapers. You can also get help with formal education, particularly for older children, through correspondence courses (see page 125), and these may include preparation for examinations of all kinds (see page 28). Some families use schools radio and TV to provide extra stimulus on a wide range of topics. (Many programmes are accompanied by pupil booklets and teacher's notes, but these must be ordered well in advance.) And some children go to evening classes in subjects of particular interest.

There's no reason why children under sixteen shouldn't go to evening classes provided the institution offering the tuition agrees. But sometimes, on the assumption that your child goes to school, you may be asked to get the head's permission. This is to make sure the classes don't interfere with normal schoolwork. Obviously it's irrelevant if your child is home educated. You are the 'head' of your 'home school', so if there's a form to fill in, it's appropriate to sign it yourself. (For discussion on doing exams at college, see page 28.)

At the outset, perhaps the best advice is to relax, be patient and think in the long term. Before you reach the right balance, you may find you need to learn and unlearn as much as your children:

> ▸ We find that the essence of a workable regime is simplicity. One or two good, colourful textbooks to guide us are enough and the rest seems to develop naturally. We have stopped driving ourselves mad trying to be too ambitious all at once and come to realise that education is a very long term and ongoing process and that consolidation is a more important factor at this stage than trendy new methods and ideas (these arise spontaneously in a lively household anyway). Though I was a teacher for so many years, I have had to unlearn a lot of cant about 'the' latest methods and 'the' essential resources and am having to learn instead a much deeper level of understanding in my relationship with my 'pupils'. Much of the equipment used in classrooms is a substitute for real life situations anyway (e.g. *playing* shops - how much better to go out and do the real thing!) I think many parents have been blinded by the educationalists' theories and believe that they do not have the necessary ability or resources to cover the ground at home. This is a myth which needs exploding, particularly at primary level.
>
> As for me - I am having to learn to relax, and I don't find that easy. All my life (being one of those so-called high powered academics) I have been expected to Achieve! As a teacher I had to achieve results and drove myself accordingly, and my pupils too. Now, I find we do the most rewarding things when I am at my most relaxed. Teaching is as much letting things happen as implanting knowledge. It requires

intuition, patience with oneself and a large measure of faith to avoid the trap of wanting to push them soullessly on towards 'goals', or pushing them on to any of the treadmills which the world considers respectable or necessary for their survival or prosperity. Time enough to make decisions when they have to drive themselves towards formal qualifications, if that is what they need for their happiness. (Short of being able to change the world overnight, this seems to be inevitable at some stage, but I hope we can make it as short and as relevant to needs as possible.) No mass institution can cater for individuals in this way - only a parent is prepared to care that much.

▸ I know I am finding my feet slowly, discovering both what the children need to know and what interests them, and learning how to use my wits to combine both factors in a good blend. I have to be patient, mostly with myself, which doesn't come easily, and be prepared to change course when I am in midstream and away and the children are still on the bank down their own private rabbit hole. To begin with I was definitely a bit paranoid about not doing it right, but now I know that no-one is breathing down my neck with terrible threats, I am beginning to relax and I am really enjoying the daily freedom to run my own life, as it used to be before the children went to school, but much more interesting in terms of activities and mobility.

Perhaps the last word should be left to a longstanding member of Education Otherwise:

▸ I have watched many EO families grow and I am struck that it is not just 'teaching children at home'. The whole family grows and develops and takes part in the excitement of learning, discovering and sharing knowledge. At its best, EO is helping to show a way of developing and of coping with our increasingly complex world. We are pioneers in a world of living and learning which far exceeds the narrow confines of a school education.

1.5 Social life

The first question people ask about home education is, 'Is it legal?' The second is, 'But what about socialisation?' This reflects the degree to which society believes that schools are essential for social learning. The implication is that if a child doesn't go to school he or she will (1) not have friends, (2) not know how to function in a group situation, and (3) not be able to cope in later life.

Schools certainly bring together large numbers of children of the same age, but what is the *quality* of this interaction, and is it always as beneficial as is assumed? According to John Holt, even its advocates are prepared to make only limited claims for it:

> When I point out to people that the social life of most schools and classrooms is mean-spirited, status-orientated, competitive and snobbish, I am always astonished by their response. Not *one* person of the hundreds with whom I've discussed this has yet said to me that the social life at school is kindly, generous, supporting, democratic, friendly, loving or good for children. No, without exception, when I condemn the social life of school, people say, 'But that's what the children are going to meet in Real Life.'*

But is this 'real life' argument actually true? Is the social life of school a bridge to the world beyond, or is it, as one EO member suggests, a cul-de-sac?

> ▸ It seems to me that the social habits acquired at school are only necessary for that particular situation - and that when one leaves it is necessary to unlearn them as rapidly as possible, which can be a painful business.

At school, peer group pressure often imposes unwritten rules such as, 'You must not have friends significantly older or younger than yourself,'

**Teach your own: a hopeful path for education*, p. 33.

or, 'You will not have friends if you appear to be particularly clever or enthusiastic'. Such rules are clearly irrelevant in the outside world. Moreover, it's certainly true that a schoolchild *can* be extremely lonely, in spite of being surrounded by a large group of peers. For many families it's the social life of the school that causes problems in the first place, and they are only too glad to forego it:

> ▸ In my opinion, schools often distort relationships between children (through fear, competition, bullying etc.). I doubt that a child who does not go misses all that much. We had a brief attempt at playgroup and we felt that the socialisation aspect was rather contrived and forced by the playgroup leaders. The discovery that he actually socialises very well with people of all ages without the 'help' of a situation like this was what finally convinced us that we could 'do it ourselves'. This is one aspect of home education that seems most to concern friends that we have talked to - the fact that the home-educated child does not spend most of his or her time in a large group of his/her peers. We have, however, come to view this as a positive advantage!
>
> When we found out about EO we still hesitated to take him out because, being an only child, we thought that the need to be with his peers was important, not realising that that, in itself, was one of his problems.

Of course many children get on perfectly well with their peers at school but they may still dislike it for other reasons. What happens when they are taken out?

> ▸ She loved being with the other kids and would have liked to go to school for playtime and lunchtime if it didn't mean going into class as well. After she came out we made a lot of effort to keep these friendships going. She maintained a couple for three years, but the lack of shared experience did make a difference. Then we moved. She joined a club to get to know local children, and she got on well with them, playing out in the street, on the rec, and sometimes in each other's flats. But gradually friendships with other home educated children have become more significant, both locally and through

national EO gatherings. These friendships tend to be based as much on personality as on age. We exchange visits as families, and increasingly we have children here on their own, and she goes off on her own. In between, she likes to have time alone to get on with her own things.

Families who choose home-based education are acutely aware of their children's needs, and in this as in other areas, they endeavour to provide for them. For some this is no problem:

▸ One criticism commonly levelled against EO parents is that children haven't the same chance to play with others freely, as do children at school. In fact, the reverse is true. As soon as school finishes one or other of Stephen's friends from the street comes calling for him, and at weekends too, they either stay at our house (sometimes eight children) or go to a friend's house... Because Stephen is not confined to the strict peer grouping of a class, his friends vary in age from six to twelve years, and with the older ones I allow him to go to the park nearby or shopping in our High Street... It appals me that several children I know have a great deal of homework for evenings and holidays even from the age of seven. But the beauty of EO is that our children are not confined in that way and will always find someone available.

▸ Most of all, we can learn to be human beings, people who have time to wonder and think about each other and the world around them. The children still meet their friends after school and in clubs and societies in the town, so that old chestnut is put firmly where it belongs! In fact, deschooled children get a chance to mix with all age groups, and learn to understand them.

▸ The advantage to us of EO is that we have a much happier son who is learning at his own pace and who is visibly gaining confidence as a person. We spend a lot of time visiting places of interest, friends and relatives, where he mixes with people of all ages, which he enjoys immensely. This, we feel, well compensates for the lack of school community life, and team and house activities, which, we were advised, would be a serious loss to him, that he hated anyway.

Out-of-school friendships are based, not on fear of rejection but on mutual respect and genuine pleasure in each other's company. They develop from choice, not necessity:

▸ Though he may have missed out academically in some respects, Andrew has broadened his horizons and become extremely mature and adult in the last six to nine months. He now has lots of friends - a few close ones, who seem to be forever drinking coffee, playing records etc.

in our house. We have long sessions talking about school and otherwise education and the system, and I find these young people all very articulate and quite passionate in their feelings that the school is not geared to their needs, but is a servant of the political and economic machine into which they are all to be thrown as obedient(?) cogs. His friends are mostly between sixteen and nineteen; some of them have left school and are suffering the bitter pangs of unemployment. I find these youngsters very practical and philosophical and much more aware than we were in my generation. They deserve more than we are giving them.

Interpersonal skills develop with practice - and a home educated child gets *more* time - not less - in the real world. Through an ordinary day they may meet and interact with children and adults of all ages and in a huge variety of situations, and will also have as their model an adult whom they trust to guide them where necessary. They will soon develop the flexibility to relate appropriately wherever they may be.

But finding the right social situation for your child is not always easy:

▸ When Michael, my nine-year-old son, spent two years out of school and stayed back with his younger brother and sister, the warmth and closeness between us was terrific. But I began to feel that his need to be at home had lived itself out; I began to feel that the situation was 'unreal' and artificial, not only for him but for my six-year-old daughter. I felt they were being deprived of the joy and excitement of going out and taking risks in other situations; of sharing their feelings with others and caring for people who are not family; of measuring themselves up against other people. I also felt in the end that they were being deprived of stimuli - not the imposed stimuli of formal teaching, but the stimuli of other people's abilities and interests and pleasure in work.

Geographical isolation, combined with remoteness from other home educating families, may make life particularly difficult:

▸ There was one difficulty we did not solve. Both Amy and James clearly began to need wider contacts than they had at home. Although they have a wide circle of friends, friendships are difficult to maintain in our isolated situation. We also felt a growing need to be able to join with others who are doing home education, and to do so on a regular basis. The children would also benefit from learning with other adults than their parents. This need became more acute when the two families with whom we met weekly for various activities moved off the island.

But rural isolation can affect schoolchildren too:

▸ For ages I wondered whether because our children didn't go to school we ought to move to an urban environment. But as I came to know more people around, whose children did go to school, I realised that the difficulties of living rurally are the same for them too when it comes to social contact. Whilst their children knew others at school, they rarely saw them at other times; no more than my children met with the friends they had made at various clubs. The actual period at school gives little time for positive socialising, only to survive what is imposed; by comparison, at our meetings with other EO families, though less frequent than school, our children's social experience was at least not one of survival! So, were our children very different from those who were at school? It seemed to me the difficulty was because we lived rurally, not because we were EOing; that rural life just does have its problems, but that they are a separate consideration from EO, in that they affect all rural-dwellers who have decided that the advantages outweigh the disadvantages, or not thought about it at all.

As our children have got older they have made friends around and cycle off to meet them. The next stage will be when they want to stay out at night - again the same for rural-dwellers at school. Unlike EOers, others take the situation for granted. So don't feel guilty about it EO-wise - just don't let folks confuse the issue!

Few home educating families work in complete isolation, and many arrange regular meetings with one another. Even where ages, circumstances and approaches differ, such meetings can be useful for social contact and moral support. Most families will be able to find others with a similar outlook who are near enough for day trips. Families who attend national gatherings of EO often strike up friendships that span the country. Often older children travel considerable distances to visit each other, living with and adapting to a new family environment:

> ▸ Many of our closest friends have been made through national meetings of EO. I wonder how many people could say that they could travel almost anywhere in the British Isles and be able to stay with friends. It's really lovely.

Even the most hardened critic, were they to see the extraordinary mix of successful relationships that can be found at an EO gathering, would have to admit that their fears are groundless. As one member wrote:

> ▸ After many years of involvement - mostly outside Britain - with home and other education alternatives, there is only one generalised comment I would apply to EO students: they tend to be socially more adaptable and outgoing - more mature - than their school-going counterparts.
>
> And this is to be expected, as EO students tend to have more open and understanding, even democratic, home environments. They also generally avoid the imposition of artificial barriers - mainly age - to social contact and can, for the most part, mix more freely and confidently with people of varying ages and backgrounds. This can make them, in a very positive way, different from their 'peers'; it is a difference which helps them to cope even better socially. And I have yet to find a neighbourhood where students - although not necessarily their parents - resented, opposed or thought EO anything other than a good thing. The standard comment directed at EO students by their school-going neighbours seems to be, 'Hey, you're lucky'.

1.6 Examinations

'What about exams?' This is perhaps the next most frequently asked question about home-based education. In the first place, are they important? This is largely a matter of personal outlook, although obviously it can also depend on what your children want to do with the rest of their lives. In general, formal qualifications may be less important than commonly supposed, and we shall return to this below. For the moment, though, we assume that your children want to do exams. Is this compatible with 'otherwise' education?

It's true that some children go back to school at fourteen specifically to do exams. But it's certainly possible to study for them at home, and for many they are just the next step to be negotiated in the course of home-based education. Indeed some children actually come *out* of school so that they can prepare for exams at home. They may even find they can get unofficial help from teachers:

> ▸ My son is currently taking GCSE courses. We have been very delighted to find that teachers from his old school (which he left because of bullying) are being extraordinarily helpful with his GCSE syllabus; and his old English teacher has come round entirely voluntarily to invigilate some of his coursework. They have also given advice, and I am amazed that they are all so dedicated, particularly to a child who has decided (- it was his decision -) to leave them. I think we should be aware that there are *some* selfless and dedicated teachers around!

You may be able to reach an agreement whereby your child goes to school for part of the time in order to do exams (see page 34). And another option that's worth considering is to enrol on an exam course at a local college. Your child may wish to wait until sixteen, but there's no reason in principle why they should have to, as long as they are mature enough to fit in with the class. (See page 20 on this point.) It has been known for children as young as eleven to go to college, but it is often seen as a preliminary step into independence at fifteen or sixteen:

▸ Leigh was home educated until nearly sixteen, then we tried to find a place for him to do his GCSEs. We were very lucky, and he was accepted at a local college. He had a very good year there, enjoyed the subjects, and fitted happily into a group of seventeen-year-olds who played snooker, drank beer and ate pizzas together at lunchtime.

The thing I was impressed with was his perseverance and organisation. His work was presented to time with few exceptions, he revised hard, tried hard, and took an interest and a pleasure in as much of the work as was compatible with human nature.

Two years ago he got his results. He did very well. His grades averaged B across the six subjects, including a C in maths. Things looked set fair for 'A' level.

Then he decided to move to the grammar school, mainly in order to avoid the long daily bus journeys. It was not a success. Unlike the college, where he had enjoyed continual development and reinforcement, the predominant experience at grammar school was one of failure, and he grew demoralised and disaffected as the year went on. By June he had decided, with our support, to leave school and look for a job as a laboratory technician.

No job materialised, but as the summer went on his confidence rebuilt itself, and he decided to return to college to restart the 'A' level course in maths, biology and English. In addition he discovered that he could take GCSE religious studies as a self-study course using correspondence texts, and having occasional tutorials with a tutor at the college.

Sally is less than eighteen months younger than Leigh. She tried secondary school at fourteen, but although the other girls went out of their way to be friendly, she hated it categorically. She stayed six weeks, and then we withdrew her.

We rather took it for granted that at sixteen she would also do a GCSE course at the college. The great unknown was how she would react to a huge place full of strange faces, the pressures of work and timetable commitments. Her situation was not as easy as Leigh's had been, as she had to do psychology there as an evening class, and maths as an evening class elsewhere, at the local community college. In our eyes, every completed week was a victory, and taking the exams the greatest achievement. In the event she was as conscientious as Leigh in attending classes, and she showed a similar capacity for becoming interested and involved in the work she had to do. She came to enjoy the college to such an extent, in fact, that she developed 'withdrawal symptoms' after the end of term.

For our first two children, going into mainstream education after home education has been a success and an achievement for them. There is a lot of difference between the cultures and styles of different institutions. The technical college environment suited Leigh and Sally, the secondary school clearly did not. The fundamental requirement of home education - the organisation of your own time and work - has produced independence and the ability to discipline themselves. The gamble seems to be paying off - we wait to see what the future will bring.

It's worth bearing in mind that a GCSE pass is of little value once you have an 'A' level in the same subject; in fact you don't need any GCSEs at all in order to enter for 'A' levels. But in any case, GCSEs and 'A' levels (in England and Wales) aren't the only possibilities. Some people choose to do the International Baccalaureate as an alternative. Other options include RSA, City and Guilds and BTEC. These are generally (but not inevitably) more vocational in nature.

If your child has acquired some degree of practical competence in a particular field of activity, they may be able to get a national vocational qualification (NVQ) in recognition of their skills. They won't have to take a formal exam, but they will need to show an assessor what they can do. They can do this either by carrying out the relevant tasks or by producing some evidence that they can do them. NVQs are being introduced progressively as a nationally recognised standard qualification, transferable from one situation to another. There are five levels, ranging roughly from below GCSE to beyond 'A' level. (For the National Council for Vocational Qualifications, see page 126.)

But if your child opts for GCSEs and decides to do them at home they will still have to choose an examining board. Here they have more choice if they are not at school. Each board has its own regulations and its own range of subjects and syllabuses, and for many subjects a single board may offer more than one alternative syllabus. It's usually a good idea to get copies of these as early as possible, and it's also advisable to get some specimen exam papers. (For initial details of examining boards try reference libraries.)

Once the decision has been made, your child will need to enter for the exam in good time. Sometimes examining boards ask for a form to be signed by the LEA. Generally this is just to assure them that children at school aren't sitting extra exams without the approval of the head. If the

LEA are uncooperative, you could simply write a statement of explanation and sign it yourself.

You will also need to be sure of the dates by which any coursework has to be submitted. When GCSEs first started there were external syllabuses with alternative papers to coursework and continuous assessment. *These have now largely gone.* External candidates can now do any exams for which they can satisfy the criteria, including any coursework. In many cases this includes submitting one or more projects of your own choice. You will need to establish who is going to moderate the work, and you may need help from the board in finding someone.

Children who don't go to school have more freedom to choose which subjects to do. They also have more flexibility in deciding when to take exams. In school the norm is for children to start a two year course at the age of fourteen for each GCSE subject they are to take. It's relatively rare for them to be taken early, although retakes and extra subjects added in the sixth form extend the age range. This can lead to six to ten subjects being taken in one go. Many pupils encountering difficulties in 'finding themselves' at this difficult age may do much worse than would otherwise be expected of them.

Home educated children can start earlier and finish later. Some will choose to take one, two or three subjects a year over a few years, studying at any one time some subjects to be taken in the current year, some at a more relaxed pace to be taken in the next year, and some for interest - perhaps to be taken in the future, perhaps never to be examined at all. This seems a good way to relieve the pressure so many schoolchildren undergo at sixteen:

> ▸ I'd like to encourage everyone with teenagers or near-teens to persevere and not send them to school on account of approaching GCSEs. If we've cracked it, anyone can.
>
> The children are very close in age and can do some subjects together and benefit from group work. We tackle an exam in an appropriate subject whenever we feel like it, and just study a range of other subjects all the time, tackling topics that seem necessary. It's important only to take an early GCSE in a subject the child is good at and knows quite a bit about already. In this way we took eight last summer (5, 2 and 1 respectively), and got good grades in all. That encouraged us to do likewise this year - but now we're on our second-best subjects!
>
> I use mostly the NEA and the SEG for boards - this ensures we get into their way of thinking and marking, limit the cost of ordering materials, and establish relationships with people at the other end. Most

people are very helpful. You need to study the rules for external candidates in case an age limit or a rule applies about attending a centre for the course. Usually there is an alternative option. The coursework, which is mostly compulsory this year, is no real obstacle and certainly removes some of the possible stress. You just have to read the marking schemes constantly and check which aims are being tested - and make sure the evidence is there in clearly labelled paragraphs. The children take a full part in this procedure once I've located the information - it makes them very responsible for their work.

Esther attended a local college for three weeks but found the students childish(!), and Julian has done both LEAG astronomy and SEG computer studies via an evening class who welcomed him. Joel has done the same exam as a private candidate from home, so either method works.

When it comes to the exam itself, no other experience is quite like sitting at a desk for up to three hours in order to write answers to a list of questions. At school many children get regular term or year exams by way of training. But given commitment and determination, exams shouldn't be a problem for home educated children after one or two practices.

But education isn't just about passing exams. People whose standard of education impresses you may turn out never to have taken any at all. Others may have done what was necessary to pass, but the joy of knowledge and achievement may have been killed in them as a result of their experience. Or they may succeed in ten subjects but learn little about life and lack insight into the time and place they live in. Examination success is very expensive if this is the price you pay for it:

▸ He decided to do three at the last minute, and got in about four months' work. He got good grades. But it was striking how all the real education stopped for the duration. Studying for exams is about learning to study for exams - it has little connection with real education.

1.7 Going back to school

It's quite common for children to return to school after being out for a while. Assuming your child is not being sent back against his or her will, there are unlikely to be any difficulties. Provided (s)he is literate and numerate, the problems of fitting in should be no different from those of transferring from one school to another.

It's better to start at the beginning of a new term, or better still at the beginning of a new school year. You can make the transfer smoother by getting an outline of the school's curriculum (which it is obliged to publish), and by looking at the school books of a neighbour's child of similar age. You may wish to check that you're up to standard with the national curriculum, but if you do have problems they are more likely to relate to the need for conformity than academic achievement.

As you can give your child more attention at home, progress in the areas you choose to cover is likely to be faster than at school, and most children who go back tend to do well:

> ▸ The twins have now been going to school for seven weeks; they are becoming fed-up, bored, disillusioned. After six years of almost no formal education they are at or near the top of their class in all those subjects they like (maths, English, music, games, nautical studies).

If you anticipate this situation you may prefer to branch out into something else rather than race ahead with subjects which will be covered at school. But if your child is enthusiastic about a particular subject, it's much more important to avoid destroying this enthusiasm than to worry about getting too far ahead.

1.8 Part time schooling

Can you send your child to school on a part time basis?

Many families would welcome an option between the extremes of full time school attendance and full time home-based education, with schools being used for selected subjects or activities. In other cases parents would simply like their children to have some experience of school as part of their overall education. Perhaps part time schooling could be a way of breaking down the monolith of compulsory school attendance, with schools taking on the role of community resource centres.

But whilst there has been a lot of interest in this idea, not all past attempts at part time schooling have been successful:

> ▸ Stephen, at six and a half, had been home educated for eighteen months when we were approached by the headmaster of a nearby school. He suggested that Stephen could attend class one morning a week, play games, and have swimming lessons at the school. He mentioned that he wanted to boost the number of pupils he had in the school. We immediately contacted the LEA, pointing out that we wished to be fully responsible for Stephen's education, and also asking them to be sure that there was sufficient provision for insurance. They agreed, by letter, to both our points.
>
> There was no doubt that Stephen enjoyed the next twelve months, attending the school part time - however, he showed no inclination to want to attend on a full time basis. Then suddenly, we received a curt note from the headmaster saying that he could no longer accept Stephen at his school because it was now full.
>
> Naturally, we were upset and sure the LEA would be sympathetic towards the fact that a seven-year-old was literally 'expelled' from school for no apparent reason. On the contrary, the LEA said that they were not covered for insurance for part time pupils - so there was nothing they could do.

Schools have often seen part time arrangements as a prelude to full time attendance. One or two LEAs have been happy to support them, but others have been cautious and obstructive:

> ▸ We recently moved to a village where the headmistress of the local school approached me and kindly offered to let James (seven) and Thomas (four) go to school for extra activities such as chess and debating and to allow them to play in the playground at lunchtime so that they could make friends. Being a village with few children, I found this an attractive proposition, so we all went along one afternoon. The

> children enjoyed it very much, so the headmistress and I began to make proper arrangements.
>
> But then the local authority reared its ugly head. When the LEA was informed, it took exception to the arrangements. I telephoned one of the underlings, a typical bureaucrat, who went round in circles trying to convince me that 'it is not Council policy' to allow children to be educated part time at school, and that if they are on roll they must be at school full time; if not on roll, then the school cannot accept responsibility for them.

School heads may be reluctant to countenance a long term arrangement without the LEA's support, but logically there is no need for the LEA to be involved (although they may be). Any 'school age' child who goes to school at all must attend regularly, but (in England and Wales) absence 'with leave' does not count as irregular attendance (Education Act 1993, s 199(3)). It is for the school to grant this leave (s 199(8)). During such absences the child is officially at school, but is effectively being 'educated off site'. (S)he is therefore covered for insurance and attracts full funding. (In Scotland the situation is less clear as there is no exact equivalent to the provision for absence 'with leave'.)

State schools in England and Wales have a duty to implement the national curriculum, and some of them may be concerned that authorised absences could interfere with its delivery. However, at least one parent has found that in practice it imposes no constraints on what is done at home. If the problem arises, the solution is to work closely with the class teacher to ensure that all elements are covered.

Arrangements for part time attendance are less likely to break down if there is some kind of formal agreement or contract with the school. The terms of such an agreement might for instance include:

- the provision that is to be made at home
- the times at which the child is expected to attend the school
- access to records and liaison with the class teacher
- participation in special events
- conditions for termination of the agreement by either side.

Part time arrangements are sometimes very successful. At one extreme, half days have always been common in reception classes, where many children find a full day too tiring. At the other, some children have done GCSEs on a part time basis, coming into school only for a meeting with each teacher, to bring in work, and to collect marked assignments and new work. This removes any problem about moderating coursework, the child takes the exams at the school, and the fees are paid as they are for full time students.

Some children go to school only for group activities like drama, choir and team sports. Others are taken out on one or two days a week for educational visits, music lessons, or just to have a freer, more peaceful period during the week:

> ▸ They are competent, independent kids, and for me that is a reward in itself. It allows me to have an interesting job for three days, and for them to do their own thing without me, and then we have a four day weekend when we share our time together and they can follow their own interests.

At its most effective, part time school attendance can enable your child to have the best of both worlds. Time spent at home allows for individual tuition and self-directed learning, whilst time at school caters for group activities and contact with peers. If the staff are flexible enough to adapt to it, it can have advantages for the school too. Teachers are freed to pay more attention to the children left behind, and if they maintain good relationships with parents it need take very little work to coordinate the child's two worlds.

For further discussion, see *Flexischooling: education for tomorrow, starting yesterday*, by Roland Meighan, available from Education Now (see page 125), price £6.00.

1.9 Bullying and school refusal

Increasingly parents are turning to home-based education because of bullying or school refusal. Often they do so out of desperation after all other solutions to the problem have been tried and failed. You should never use the threat of withdrawing your child from school simply as a ploy to exert pressure on the authorities. On the other hand, many families who are driven to home education in these circumstances find that it works, often to their own surprise and delight:

> ▸ I never planned to teach Angela at home - it happened by accident. Things had got to the stage where she just wouldn't go to school - she was really distressed even at the mention of it. The EWO was calling her naughty and spoilt and threatening to drag her there. Then the LEA threatened to take me to court and to apply for a care order. In the end I saw red. I said I'd teach her myself and sent the EWO packing. I hadn't meant to say it, but it suddenly came to me that I'd read an article about home education in the local paper. I went to the library and got them to find me an address for Education Otherwise. Since then we never looked back. We've been home educating ever since and Angela's doing fine.

If your child is being bullied

Bullying at school can be stopped provided the teachers, especially the head, have the will to take action. The Anti-Bullying Campaign (ABC), set up under the auspices of Kidscape (see page 125), can give practical guidance on how to manage this, along with many examples of how quickly it can be done.

But what if the will isn't there? Typically the head insists, 'We don't have a problem with bullying in this school.' It's worth taking the issue to

> Parents are occasionally browbeaten into allowing their children to be drugged or hospitalised as 'treatment' for school refusal. They are usually told that the alternative is a care order until the child is nineteen. If this is said to you, ask for it to be put into writing (it won't be), and get support at once. Remember you don't have to allow your child to be given drugs to get them to go to school. No-one has to agree to medical treatment they do not want.

the PTA, the governors, the LEA and the education committee - in some areas they have put a lot of work into it. But unless a substantial number of complaints have been made, there's a limit to what they can do if the head is adamant. And if, as sometimes happens, the bullying is being done by a teacher rather than by children, this could make things much harder.

If you aren't sure how seriously to take the problem, ABC can help you get some perspective on it. Some children can be helped to see how they provoke teasing, or can learn to stand up for themselves through self-assertion classes or martial arts. But too often children are expected to put up with treatment which adults would never tolerate, and are made to feel it is their fault. On the contrary, many are happy, gifted children from secure homes, and are not provocative. The bully is invariably from an insecure home, and case histories indicate that the disturbance shows up early and, unless treated, continues into disturbed adult relationships.

Much bullying is serious abuse. Any injuries should be shown to the GP, so there is a medical record, and you should take photographs of them. Physical attacks should be reported to the police in the same way as if an adult had been attacked. A child should not be left in school to endure this sort of treatment, and the best course of action may be to withdraw them. Even if you aren't sure you want to home educate permanently, you can take them out while you try to resolve the problem. There's no reason why you shouldn't do this, so long as you explain your intentions and make sure your child is properly educated (see pages 51, 59 and 78).

School refusal

Parents of school refusers are often told that their child is unique. No-one else has this problem, and of course it's all their fault. In fact school refusal is quite a common phenomenon, and there are well established views on what causes it and how to deal with it. Supposedly the problem is a more or less intractable one (possibly a phobia similar to agoraphobia and claustrophobia), and it is invariably caused by 'separation anxiety' on the part of the mother. According to this doctrine, 'school phobic children should never be educated at home',* and the only way to deal with it is to force the child back into school immediately so that no rewards like having a pleasant day at home reinforce such bad behaviour.

*Ian Berg, in *Out of school,* edited by L. Hersov and I. Berg, Wiley, 1981

Ian Berg did this, and he followed up a hundred of his former patients for three years. At the end of this period, a third of them were functioning normally in terms of social adjustment and work or further education. Another third were mildly neurotic, and the remaining third were severely disturbed. He considered this to be a successful outcome in the circumstances. Without subscribing to this view it has been difficult to get a job as a psychologist or psychotherapist in an NHS or local authority facility dealing with school refusers. This closed shop has in turn tended to perpetuate the 'school phobia' myth. Although we have begun to hear of more sympathetic treatment recently, many health care workers are still very punitive towards school refusing children.

But Education Otherwise now knows of enough school refusers who have been withdrawn from school to start compiling statistics of its own. Some of these children may simply have been refusing school as a rational and healthy response to an intolerable situation; others may have been suicidal, with additional problems such as agoraphobia, violent behaviour, anorexia, etc. So far almost all of them have come to function well in terms of learning effectively and mixing well in the community, often remarkably soon after being taken out of school:

> ▸ She gets up at seven to go to work, and she's singing. She's got a steady boyfriend. I wouldn't have believed it possible those two years when she was suicidal and running away.

> ▸ I'm going to college for 'A' levels - astronomy, physics and maths - and I love it. There's a counsellor I can go and talk to if I'm worried; but everyone's so nice. I can go out anywhere with no problem. All that other stuff's like a bad dream.

> ▸ He couldn't do any 'school' subjects when he came out - he seemed thick. But he could write really sophisticated pieces on photography and how cameras work. He was just blocked on anything he associated with school. The careers officer said he'd have to do YTS because he couldn't possibly get a job in photography without qualifications, but he got a job easily in a small studio. All they wanted was enthusiasm and someone who would do as they were told. He came to life on the day he was sixteen and started work, and knew he was safe from school. He's moved on to a very good job now, and he has his own dark room at home, and girls begging him to take professional portraits - great for his social life.

For further discussion of bullying and school refusal, see *Troubled children: a fresh look at school phobia* and *The abuse of care and custody orders and understanding school phobia*, both by Patricia Knox and available from Education Otherwise.

2

The law relating to the education of children out of school

2.1 The right to 'otherwise' education

Everyone is entitled to education. This principle is contained in both the United Nations Universal Declaration of Human Rights (article 26) and the European Convention on Human Rights (article 2 of Protocol no.1). But what about the right to freedom of choice in education? Article 26(3) of the UN Declaration states:

> Parents have a prior right to choose the kind of education that shall be given to their children.

And according to the European Convention:

> In the exercise of any function which it assumes in relation to education and to teaching, the state shall respect the right of parents to ensure such education and teaching is in conformity with their own religious and philosophical convictions.

Unlike the UN Declaration, the European Convention has the force of law. But could it actually be invoked in defence of the right to educate at home? This is by no means clear. German domestic law does not allow education otherwise than at school. A recent attempt was made to challenge this under the Convention, but the application (by Renata Leuffen against the Federal Republic of Germany, 1992) was rejected by the European Commission of Human Rights. The Commission took the view that article 2 of Protocol no. 1 did not prevent the state from establishing compulsory schooling, provided it did not pursue an aim of indoctrination.

So what gives parents the right to educate their children out of school? To find an explicit reference to this, we need to turn to national law. For England and Wales, the general principle of parental choice is set out in s 76 of the Education Act 1944:

> In the exercise and performance of all powers and duties conferred and imposed on them by the Education Acts 1944 to 1993 the Secretary of State for Education, the funding authorities and local education authorities shall have regard to the general principle that, so far as is compatible with the provision of efficient instruction and training and the avoidance of unreasonable public expenditure, pupils are to be educated in accordance with the wishes of their parents.

But the specific right to home educate stems from s 36 of the same Act:

> It shall be the duty of the parent of every child of compulsory school age to cause him to receive efficient full-time education suitable to his age, ability and aptitude, and to any special educational needs he may have, either by regular attendance at school or otherwise.

For home educators, the two words 'or otherwise' are probably the most important ones in English law. Because of them, parents can choose

For Scotland, the principle of parental choice is set out in s 28(1) of the Education (Scotland) Act 1980:

> In the exercise and performance of their powers and duties under this Act the Secretary of State [for Scotland] and education authorities shall have regard to the general principle that, so far as is compatible with the provision of suitable instruction and training and the avoidance of unreasonable public expenditure, pupils are to be educated in accordance with the wishes of their parents.

The right to educate otherwise than at school is contained in s 30 of the same Act:

> It shall be the duty of the parent of every child of school age to provide efficient education for him suitable to his age, ability and aptitude either by causing him to attend a public school regularly or by other means.

(Because of a slight divergence from the phrasing of the English Act, the words 'by other means' apply to all kinds of private education, including education at a private school.)

The legal information on the following pages is meant for general guidance only. Although we have done our best to see that it is accurate, inevitably we have had to simplify and leave things out. You should also bear in mind that the law changes from time to time.

If you have a particular problem of any complexity we suggest you refer to the legislation itself. If appropriate you may also wish to consider seeing a solicitor (see page 118).

whether to delegate their children's education to a school or carry it out themselves.

The rights of children

Many people would feel that children themselves should play as large a part as practicable in deciding whether to embark on 'otherwise' education. Nevertheless the legal responsibility for education lies entirely with the parent. Under English (and Scottish) law, children have a right to education, but no right to choose or influence what form it takes. There is no legal requirement that parents, schools or education authorities should accede to their wishes or preferences. The only explicit references to a child's wishes concern care orders and education supervision orders (see page 54). Here the authority has a duty to find out these wishes and take them into account.

2.2 The duty of the parent in English law

Now we can look at s 36 of the 1944 Act in detail. This is essentially what it says:

- If you have a *school-age* child, you must see that (s)he is *educated.*
- You can delegate this duty to a school, or you can carry it out yourself.
- In any case, the education provided must be *efficient* and *full-time*.
- It must be *suitable to the child's age, ability and aptitude*.
- If your child has *special educational needs*, it must cater for them.

What exactly does this mean? Nowhere in the 1944 Act or in subsequent legislation is the term *education* defined. Most of the other terminology in s 36 is not defined either. For many of these expressions our only source of guidance is an appeal case which was brought to Worcester Crown Court in 1981 (Harrison & Harrison v Stevenson). In this case the judge defined *education* as 'the development of mental powers and character and the acquisition of knowledge through the imparting of skills and learning by systematic instruction'. He went on to describe an *efficient* system of education as one which 'achieves that which it sets out to achieve'. Finally, he defined education as *suitable* if it is such as

1. to prepare the children for life in modern civilised society; and
2. to enable them to achieve their full potential.

This definition is a very general one and could encompass a variety of educational styles and methods. Education Otherwise defends the right of families to take direct responsibility for their children's education regardless of the particular approach they wish to adopt. But for all its broadness, the judge's definition does set limits. There are some parents who, for whatever reason, see home education as a means of separating their children from society at large. In taking this view they may fail to meet the first of these criteria, and EO would find it difficult to support them in any conflict with the authorities.

With respect to the second criterion, critics sometimes claim that children are denied opportunities by being kept away from school. But many parents choose to educate their children at home precisely because they feel they are giving them *more* freedom, not less, to become everything they are capable of becoming, and thereby to improve the quality of society for everyone.

The terms *school-age*, *full-time* and *special educational needs* will be discussed below. Apart from this, the important thing to know is that this is *all* there is to be said about your duty. *Provided your child is not a registered pupil at a school* (see page 51), you are bound by no other constraints. In particular:

- You don't need permission to educate 'otherwise'.
- You don't have to tell the LEA (but see page 49 on this point).
- You don't have to have premises equipped to any particular standard.
- You don't have to be a qualified teacher.
- You don't have to cover the same syllabus as the school.
- You don't have to follow the national curriculum (see page 92).
- You don't have to plan your curriculum in advance at all.
- You don't have to keep to school hours, days or terms.
- You don't need a fixed timetable.
- You don't have to give formal school-type lessons in a classroom.

You may well *choose* to do any or all of these things, but you don't *have* to. You need to be able to show, if required, that you are serious about home-based education and that you are offering your child a reasonably wide range of appropriate opportunities (some of which may well be declined!). If your child is happy, healthy, and is responding well to what you are providing, the chances are that your educational arrangements are 'suitable'. If (s)he is bored, resistant, frustrated or badly behaved, you may need to think again.

In order to be efficient, your education does not have to cover the same syllabus as the equivalent education being offered in school, nor does it

A longer statement of educational aims can be found in Article 29 of the UN Convention on the Rights of the Child, ratified by the UK in 1991. Article 29 prescribes that education shall be directed to:

- the development of the child's personality, talents and mental and physical abilities to their fullest potential;
- the development of respect for human rights and fundamental freedoms, and for the principles enshrined in the Charter of the United Nations;
- the development of respect for the child's parents, his or her own cultural identity, language and values, for the national values of the country in which the child is living, the country from which he or she may originate, and for civilizations different from his or her own;
- the preparation of the child for responsible life in a free society, in the spirit of understanding, peace, tolerance, equality of sexes, and friendship among all peoples, ethnic, national and religious groups and persons of indigenous origin;
- the development of respect for the natural environment.

have to meet any hypothetical standard set by any school or the authority (Bevan v Shears, 1911, 2KB 936). So long as it is full-time, education can take place anywhere and at any time. So long as it is suitable for your child, it can take any form. As for the definition of 'efficient education' quoted above, it has been wryly pointed out that if all education had to achieve what it set out to achieve, every child who failed to benefit from school would put their parents in breach of the law!

School age

The expression *compulsory school age* is of course a misleading shorthand, and should not be taken to imply that school itself is compulsory. It simply means the age at which *education* is compulsory. In England and Wales this is any age between the fifth and sixteenth birthdays (1944 Act, s 35, as amended by the Raising of the School Leaving Age Order 1972 (S.I. 1972/444)). But this will change if and when s 277 of the Education Act 1993 is brought into force.

Under the old law, if your home educated child is sixteen today and has not been a registered pupil at a school for at least a year, you have no further legal duty to provide education. If they wish to start work, they may do so straight away, and do not need to wait until the appropriate school leaving date. But if they have been a registered pupil at a school at any time after their fifteenth birthday, the situation is slightly more complicated. In these circumstances education must continue until the appropriate school leaving date. This is either Easter (September-January birthdays) or May (February-August birthdays) (Education Act 1962, s 9, as amended by the Education (School-leaving dates) Act 1976).

Under the new law there will be a single school leaving date in each year. 'Compulsory school age' will be any age between the fifth birthday and whichever school leaving date falls within the same school year as the sixteenth birthday. *There will no longer be any distinction between school pupils and home educated children in this respect* (Education Act 1993, s 277). (Phone the LEA office if you need to check whether this has come into force.)

Full-time

There is no agreed definition of this term. In 1987 the average time spent on teaching in England and Wales was 22½ hours a week in state primary schools and 24 hours in state secondary schools. However, these figures are statistics only and have no legal force. In any case they are not really relevant to home education, which generally takes place on a one-to-one basis in very different conditions.

Under s 298(4) of the Education Act 1993, LEAs may provide home tuition for certain children. The DFEE (formerly the DFE) advises that 'the appropriate number of hours of direct tuition may differ according to the needs of the pupil', but that 'pupils should also be set work to do on their own outside periods of direct contact' (circular 11/94, May 1994, paragraph 70). The Department's earlier advice was that a *maximum* of ten hours' tuition a week should be provided for children of eight and over, and this was sometimes used by LEAs to demand 'ten hours a week of qualified tuition'. There is no legal basis for such a demand.

For the purpose of withholding social security payments, the DSS considers attendance at college of twelve hours or more per week as 'full-time'.

There is some scope for ambiguity in the use of the term *education.* Does it mean *learning, studying* or *teaching*? Some home educators argue that education takes place throughout their children's waking hours, and that any discussion of the meaning of 'full-time' is therefore superfluous. In this connection, see the letter on page 88.

Special educational needs

These words were inserted into s 36 of the 1944 Act in 1981. The current English legislation on special educational needs is contained in Part III of the Education Act 1993. Section 156 of the 1993 Act defines 'special educational needs' in terms of 'a learning difficulty which calls for special educational provision to be made'. The Act provides for a 'statement of special educational needs' to be made if appropriate. Any such statement includes a definition of these needs as assessed by the LEA. The LEA must also say in the statement what special educational provision they propose to make to meet them, but this does not prevent you from making your own alternative provision otherwise than at school. This topic is discussed in detail below, beginning on page 60.

2.3 The duty of the local education authority in England and Wales

In England and Wales the level of local government responsible for education is known as a *local education authority* (LEA). The *education committee* of the council is made up of elected representatives and determines general policy, subject to statutory requirements. The staff of the *education department* (see boxes on pages 74 to 76) are paid to carry out this policy.

As a parent you have the main responsibility for seeing that your child is educated. The chief function of the LEA is to provide and maintain schools. But the LEA also have a duty, in case of doubt, to see that you discharge your parental responsibility properly. This duty of the LEA is set out in s 192 of the Education Act 1993, which begins:

> If it appears to a local education authority that a child of compulsory school age in their area is not receiving suitable education, either by regular attendance at school or otherwise, they shall serve a notice in writing on the parent...

This doesn't say you have to tell the LEA you are educating 'otherwise'. Discussing a home educating family, one junior LEA officer was heard to remark, 'They didn't tell us they were educating their child out of school, but we're on to them now.' This attitude is quite wrong, and when the EO local coordinator complained about it the LEA apologised. Without going out of their way to be secretive, many home educating families make no attempt to contact the LEA and are left undisturbed. *Provided your child is not a registered pupil at a state school* (see page 51), you need not worry that this will put you in a worse position if you should somehow come to the LEA's notice. Don't be apologetic - just be cool and confident. Explain that you were under no legal obligation to tell them, but that if they wish to satisfy themselves they are welcome to do so.

If you come to their notice, many LEAs will consider it their duty to make enquiries. Others may prefer to turn a blind eye to a problem which is likely to entail more work and divert their energies away from children who may be in need of more urgent attention. It is arguable how active their role should be in monitoring home education. As one parent has put it, s 192 implies that 'the LEA should only intervene if it believes there is something amiss'. But this view has been shown to be too extreme: case law has established that LEAs are entitled to ask you informally for information, even though they may have no reason to suppose at this stage that you are not educating properly (Phillips v Brown, 20 June 1980). You are not legally obliged to provide the information they ask for; but if you fail to respond they could quite reasonably conclude that you seem not to be educating properly, and they would then have to take action.

If the LEA think you may not be educating properly, the formal steps they should take are laid down in s 192-198 of the 1993 Act. LEAs don't often embark on this procedure, but it is summarised here for reference:

1. They serve you with a notice giving you at least two weeks to satisfy them that you are educating properly.

2. If you fail to satisfy them, they then have to consider whether it is expedient for your child to go to school. If they think it is, they must serve you with a 'school attendance order'. But before they do this they serve you with a second notice telling you which school they intend to name in it and giving you the chance to choose an alternative.
3. They serve you with a school attendance order requiring you to register your child as a pupil at the school named in it.
4. At this point you can still ask them to revoke the order because you are educating 'otherwise'. (Alternatively you can ask them to amend it because your child has been offered a place at a different school, but this option is unlikely to be relevant.)
5. If they refuse to revoke the order, you can appeal to the Secretary of State.
6. If you don't comply with the order they can take you to court, but you will still have the opportunity to show the court that you are educating 'otherwise'. (See also page 54 for other steps they may take.)

You have the opportunity, both before and after you are served with a school attendance order, to give evidence of your education. If the LEA have visited you, the best thing to do may be to ask them for a copy of the inspector's report (if you have not had one) and a full explanation of why they are not satisfied. In the meantime you would be wise to start preparing a report of your own on what you are doing. If you are a member of EO you may find it useful to discuss things with your local coordinator and/or other experienced members.

If the LEA reply cooperatively you can respond by submitting your report, taking care to incorporate answers to their criticisms. At this point it would be reasonable to expect them to halt the procedure, acknowledge your report, and reassess your provision in the light of it. If they refuse to say why they aren't satisfied, you should send your report in any case, but you may want to consider going to the local ombudsman at this point (page 114), particularly if they have behaved unreasonably in other ways.

But this situation doesn't often arise. Usually the LEA will simply contact you informally from time to time to check that you seem to be educating sensibly. Typically they will want to visit your home, talk to you and your child, and look at any work and resources (see page 97). Most families find this reasonable provided the inspector makes an acceptable appointment, establishes a friendly relationship with the child, and sends a copy of their report immediately afterwards (page 106). But the choice of how to satisfy the LEA lies with you, and there are other possibilities (page 86). Home visits usually turn out to be the easiest one: if you prefer to satisfy the LEA by other means you may find you have to work harder (page 103).

2.4 Withdrawing your child from school in England and Wales

If you have a 'school-age' child, s 36 of the 1944 Act says you must see that (s)he is educated. But if the child is a registered pupil at a school, you have an extra duty under s 199 of the 1993 Act to make sure (s)he attends regularly. This is the section used against truancy. Subject to certain statutory excuses, if you fail in this duty you are guilty of a criminal offence and may be taken to court. (See also page 54 for other steps the LEA may take.) Technically it makes no difference in this situation whether or not you are providing education out of school.

What is a registered pupil at a school? The registration of pupils is provided for by the Education (Pupil Registration) Regulations 1995 (S.I. 1995/2089). Regulation 5 requires schools to keep admission and attendance registers. A child whose name is on the school admission register is a registered pupil. The presence or absence at school of registered pupils is recorded in the attendance register. A child will not be registered simply because you have put their name down for a school, but as soon as you actually send them there you can assume that they are. At this point your duty to secure regular attendance begins. (But note that it only applies if your child is of 'compulsory school age'. So if you have a four-year-old at school, you are not committed to sending them regularly and can withdraw them without formality.)

If you are withdrawing your child from school it is important to see that (s)he is deregistered. The grounds on which a pupil's name must be deleted

Travellers and school attendance

If you need to travel about in the course of trade or business, you only have to send the child to school as regularly as the trade or business permits. Once the child is six this is subject to a minimum of 200 (half-day) attendances in any twelve month period (i.e. about 50% attendance) (1993 Act, s 199(6)).

Whether the child is going to school or not at any particular time, you still have a duty (under s 36 of the 1944 Act) to provide suitable education.

from the admission register are listed in regulation 9. Under regulation 9(1)(c), a 'school-age' pupil's name is to be deleted from the admission register if:

> ... he has ceased to attend the school and the proprietor has received written notification from the parent that the pupil is receiving education otherwise than at school.

This means you need to write to the head explaining clearly that you are educating the child at home (see page 78). The head must then take the child's name off the register, and is also obliged (under regulation 13(3)) to inform the LEA within two weeks. Once the head gets your letter, your duty to secure regular attendance comes to an end (although you can still be prosecuted for any periods of unauthorised absence which took place before that). Of course you have a continuing obligation to provide education, and you can now expect the LEA to ask you about your arrangements.

Before September 1995 the situation was different. Parents had to satisfy the LEA that proper education was taking place *before* the child's name could be taken off the register. If the LEA were not satisfied, they could prosecute for irregular attendance without having to show that the education was inadequate. But now it no longer makes any difference whether you have just withdrawn your child from a state school or not. In either case you ultimately have the right to defend the adequacy of your arrangements in court.

Under the old regulations, case law had established that before prosecuting for irregular attendance LEAs should give families enough time to start home educating, and enough chance to show that they were doing

Other grounds for deregistration of 'school-age' pupils include:

- The child is now at another school (apart from a pupil referral unit or, in some circumstances, a special school).
- The child has moved too far away from the school to get there easily.
- The child was at a private school but has now stopped going to it.
- The child has been permanently excluded (i.e. expelled) from a state school, and a decision has been taken not to reinstate him/her.

(In addition to the above, it seems reasonable to assume that your child is no longer a registered pupil when (s)he has come to the end of primary or middle school.)

So for instance, if you have just moved to another area but have not yet sent your child to school there, you have no further duty to secure attendance under s 199 of the 1993 Act. And if your child is at a non-state school, all you have to do to remove their name from the register is tell the school that you intend to stop sending them (but see also page 81).

it properly (R v Gwent County Council ex parte Perry, CA 10 July 1985). Although the regulations have changed, this judgement could still prove relevant if LEAs rush into the school attendance order procedure without first allowing sufficient time and opportunity for informal enquiries.

Whilst the new regulations are clearly fairer than the old ones, they are still less than perfect. Regulation 9(2) provides that in many situations, including withdrawal in order to educate at home, a child cannot be deregistered from a special school without the LEA's consent. The ostensible purpose of this restriction is to protect the child's interests, but it could provide an excuse for discrimination and prejudice if invoked inappropriately.

2.5 Education supervision orders and care proceedings in England and Wales

If you can find out all about home education before you start doing it, you are unlikely to have any legal difficulties. But what if you have suddenly been thrown into 'otherwise' education as a result of a crisis? You may already be involved in legal proceedings simply through lack of information. In this case you would be well advised to join Education Otherwise immediately, contact your local coordinator, and get as much support and advice as you can find.

LEAs can prosecute parents for two offences under the 1993 Act. One is failing to comply with a school attendance order (s 198; see page 50); the other is not seeing that your child goes to school regularly (s 199; see page 51). But whether they do this or not, the LEA also have a duty to consider applying for an *education supervision order* under s 36 of the Children Act 1989. And in the course of proceedings under the 1993 Act, the court itself may direct the LEA to apply for such an order (1993 Act, s 202). Nevertheless, the LEA are unlikely to apply for an education supervision order without your cooperation, and you should think carefully before agreeing, even if the alternative is prosecution under s 198 or s 199.

Education supervision orders (ESOs) were introduced in 1991 as a more appropriate response to truancy than care orders. Their effect is to suspend your rights and duties under the 1944 and 1993 Acts and to transfer responsibility for the child's education to a supervisor. The supervisor has to 'advise, assist and befriend' you and your child. (S)he also has to give directions to you both, but must first try to find out your respective wishes and feelings in order to take these into account. These include 'wishes as to the place at which the child should be educated'. (This wording was adopted following representations from EO. Since the word 'school' is not used, 'otherwise' education is not ruled out.)

Before applying for an ESO, the LEA have to consult the social services department. If there are non-educational grounds for concern, this could result in a care order being made instead.

Before it makes an ESO, the court must be satisfied that your child is not being properly educated (as defined by s 36 of the 1944 Act - see page 42). This will normally give you a chance to show that your arrangements are suitable - how easy this turns out to be will depend to a large extent on what has already happened.

Once an ESO has been made, you and your child have to comply with the supervisor's directions. If you persistently and unreasonably fail to do so, you could be prosecuted. In the child's case, this could lead to care proceedings. The order may require your child to allow visits and to keep the supervisor informed of any change of address. In any case, if the child is living with you, you have to allow the supervisor reasonable contact, and if you know where the child is living you have to tell the supervisor if asked.

In due course, you or your child may apply to the court to have an ESO discharged. You might want to do this, for instance, if, with the supervisor's agreement, you have successfully embarked on 'otherwise' education in the meantime.

To make a care order under the Children Act, the court must be satisfied that the child is suffering, or likely to suffer, 'significant harm', and that the order will improve matters (s 31). 'Harm' includes, among other things, the impairment of intellectual development.

2.6 The law in Scotland

The duty of the parent

The parent's duty to provide education is set out in Section 30 of the Education (Scotland) Act 1980 (quoted on page 42). This is what it says:

- If you have a *school-age* child, you must see that (s)he is *educated.*
- You can do this either by sending the child to a state school or by other means.
- In any case, the education provided must be *efficient.*
- It must also be *suitable to the child's age, ability and aptitude.*

The terms *education*, *efficient* and *suitable* are not defined. The definitions given in the Harrison case (page 44) could be of interest here, although they would not necessarily carry much weight in Scotland. *School age* is defined by s 31-33 of the 1980 Act. Compulsory education begins on the next 'school commencement date' after the child's fifth birthday. It ends on a 'school leaving date' near to the child's sixteenth birthday. School commencement dates are fixed locally. The school leaving dates are the last day of May (March-September birthdays) and (for children not attending school) 21 December (October-February birthdays).

The main thing to note is how *little* the law says about your duty. *Provided your child is not at school* you are bound by no other constraints. (See page 45 for the list of things you don't have to do).

The role of the education authority

Unless you are taking your child out of a state school (see page 59), you don't have to tell the education authority you are educating 'by other means'; but once they know about you they are entitled to investigate. Usually this should just be a matter of checking up informally on your arrangements.

Many people educate their children at home with the full cooperation of the education authority. But sometimes conflicts develop. The authority have a duty to take action if they are 'not satisfied' that you are educating your 'school age' child properly. The formal steps they should take are laid down in s 37-41 of the 1980 Act, summarised here for reference:

1. They serve you with a notice giving you at least a week to provide whatever information they ask for about your arrangements. You can choose whether to do this in person (with or without the child) or in writing.

2. If you fail to satisfy them *either* that you are educating properly *or* that you have 'reasonable excuse' for not doing, they must make an 'attendance order'. But before they do this they must consider any views you have expressed about the school you want your child to go to.

3. They serve you with an attendance order requiring you to send your child to the school named in it.

4. Once the order is served, you have two weeks to appeal to the sheriff, who may confirm, vary or annul it.

5. You can ask the education authority to revoke the order because you have made alternative arrangements (including arrangements for home education). (Alternatively you can ask them to amend it by substituting another school which has agreed to accept your child.)
6. If they won't do this, or if they fail to decide within a month, you can appeal to the sheriff.
7. If you don't comply with the order you can be taken to court, but you won't be guilty if you can show that you have a 'reasonable excuse'. (Under s 44(1), whether it convicts you or not, if the court finds that there was irregular attendance without reasonable excuse it can refer the case to the local authority reporter. See box on page 58.)

If you find yourself enmeshed in these formal procedures the same remarks apply as for England and Wales (see page 50). But in practice this situation doesn't often arise, as most conflicts are resolved informally.

'Reasonable excuse'

This concept appears in the 1980 Act in connection with both failure to educate and irregular attendance. 'Reasonable excuse' can be any of the following (s 42):

- No school within 'walking distance' will educate the child free of charge, and the education authority have made no arrangements for travel, boarding or tutoring.
- The child is ill. (In this case the education authority have the right to insist on medical examination.)
- There are other circumstances constituting a reasonable excuse in the opinion of the education authority or the court.

If you have applied for an attendance order to be revoked or amended, this is not in itself a reasonable excuse for failing to attend the school named in it.

Children's hearings

As a parent you can be prosecuted for two offences under the 1980 Act. One is failing to comply with an attendance order (s 41); the other is failing to secure regular attendance (s 35). But whether they prosecute you for irregular attendance or not, the education authority may refer your child to the local authority reporter. And whether or not it convicts you of either offence, if a court finds that there was irregular attendance without reasonable excuse it can also refer the case to the local authority reporter. This is not likely to happen very often, but the possibility is there, and the following brief summary is given for reference. If your child *is* referred to the local authority reporter you would be well advised to seek legal advice if you have not done so already.

Under s 39 of the Social Work (Scotland) Act 1968, the reporter may

1. decide that no further action is needed; or
2. refer the child and family to the local authority for advice, guidance and assistance; or
3. conclude that conditions are met whereby your child seems to need compulsory care. (One of these conditions is irregular school attendance without reasonable excuse.)

In the third of these cases the reporter must get a report from the local authority and convene a hearing before the children's panel, which you and your child must normally both attend (s 40-41).

The procedure at children's hearings is set out in s 42-44 of the Act. The chairman starts by explaining the grounds for referral. (If you or your child do not accept them, the reporter must apply to the sheriff for a decision on whether they exist. The chairman must tell you about this.) After considering the report and any other evidence, the panel can decide

1. that no further action is needed; or
2. to adjourn pending further investigation (- this could entail taking the child away for assessment); or
3. to make a supervision requirement (i.e. a residential or non-residential care order).

Under s 48-50 you have three weeks to appeal to the sheriff against the panel's decision, and where a supervision requirement has been made you can apply to the panel for the requirement to be suspended pending your appeal. After that you have a further four weeks to appeal against the sheriff's decision to the Court of Session on a point of law. Supervision requirements must be reviewed at least once a year, and may be reviewed after a shorter period if you or your child ask for it.

Withdrawing your child from school

How do you go about withdrawing your child from school? Section 35(1) of the 1980 Act provides that:

> Where a child of school age who has attended a public school on one or more occasions fails without reasonable excuse to attend regularly at the said school, then, unless the education authority have consented to the withdrawal of the child from the school (which consent shall not be unreasonably withheld), his parent shall be guilty of an offence against this section.

This suggests that the safest course of action is to seek the education authority's consent while your child is still going to school.

But experience to date shows that authorities are very reluctant to give their consent in this situation, and you could be kept waiting indefinitely. So can you begin to educate at home in the meantime?

Education (Scotland) Act 1980, s 36: Irregular attendance at a state school

If the education authority think you have failed to see that your child attends regularly, they must serve you with a notice giving you at least 48 hours to explain the child's absence in person (with or without the child). If you are unable to satisfy them that you have a reasonable excuse, they may either prosecute you straight away or warn you and wait for up to six weeks before deciding whether to prosecute or not. In the latter case they can make an attendance order. (Before they do this they must consider any views you have expressed about the school you want your child to go to. The rest of the procedure is set out in points 3-7 on page 56.)

Whether they prosecute you or not, the education authority may refer your child to the local authority reporter (see page 58). Likewise (under s 44), if you *are* taken to court, and if the court finds there was irregular attendance without reasonable excuse, it may refer the case to the reporter regardless of whether it convicts you as well. Alternatively the court may itself make an attendance order.

A barrister was asked on behalf of EO whether the intention to educate by other means could count *in itself* as 'reasonable excuse' for irregular attendance. He felt this was unlikely, but went on to say that

> while I am of opinion that a bare declaration of intention to educate the child at home would not be reasonable excuse, the fact that the child was being afforded at home an education which was efficient and suitable to his age, ability and aptitude would, if established, in my opinion constitute reasonable excuse.

In other words a court would probably not think it was reasonable to keep your child away from school simply because you *wished* to home educate, but it might well conclude that you had behaved reasonably if you could show that you *had been* educating appropriately.

Even if you take your child out of school before obtaining the authority's consent, you would be wise to write to them to explain what you are doing. Otherwise they will be more likely to embark on the formal truancy procedure (see box on page 59). But if they do start this procedure, they may still accept evidence of suitable ongoing home education as sufficient explanation of the child's absence.

If they don't accept your explanation they can take you to court for irregular attendance. You will then need to convince the court in turn that:

1. you were providing suitable education for your child; and
2. this constitutes reasonable excuse for irregular attendance.

For more on taking your child out of school, see page 81.

2.7 Children with 'special educational needs' in England and Wales

Special educational needs are defined in s 156 of the Education Act 1993 in terms of 'a learning difficulty which calls for special educational provision to be made'. A child has a learning difficulty if:

- (s)he has a significantly greater difficulty in learning than most children of the same age; or
- (s)he has a disability which prevents or hinders him/her from making use of educational facilities generally provided in local schools for children of the same age.

By this definition it was thought that about 20% of pupils might have special educational needs at some time in their school careers.

Part III of the Act imposes certain duties on LEAs. If an LEA think that

- a child has (or probably has) special educational needs, and
- it is necessary (or is probably necessary) to decide what special educational provision these needs call for,

they first have to make an *assessment* of those needs (s 167). If in the light of this assessment they still need to decide what provision is called for, they then have to make a *statement of special educational needs* (s 168).

At the same time, the Act gives you certain rights as a parent. You have the right:

- to be given formal notice if the LEA intend to make an assessment;
- to be given information about the assessment procedure;
- to be given at least four weeks to make representations and submit written evidence;
- to be present at examinations which are part of the assessment;
- to be notified after the assessment of whether the LEA intend to make a statement of special educational needs;
- to be given a copy of the draft statement, including copies of the reports of the examinations;
- to make further representations or meet advisers;
- to be given the name of an officer who can provide further information.

> The law relating to children with special educational needs in England and Wales is contained in the Education Act 1993 Part III and Schedules 9-11, together with the Education (Special Educational Needs) Regulations 1994 (SI 1994/1047). In addition, a code of practice exists giving guidance to LEAs and school governors.

In making an assessment the LEA must seek the following advice:

- *Advice from the parent.*
- *Educational advice:* This must normally be given by the head of each school the child has attended during the last eighteen months. Heads who have not personally taught the child must consult a teacher who has.
- *Medical advice:* This must be sought from a fully qualified medical practitioner ('school doctor'), designated by the district health authority.
- *Psychological advice* from the LEA's educational psychologist, who must consult with any other psychologist who has 'relevant knowledge'.
- *Advice from the social services authority*
- Any other advice which they consider appropriate.

If they decide to make a statement of special educational needs, they must follow strict guidelines on its content and form, and they must inform and guide you on your rights of appeal. A statement must specify:

1. the child's special educational needs;
2. the special educational provision considered appropriate to meet those needs;
3. appropriate school or other arrangements;
4. any non-educational provision to be made.

All the reports, evidence and advice must be appended, including that provided by the parents.

Statements must be reviewed at least once a year.

This is only a very broad outline of the law relating to 'special' children. Some of its implications for 'otherwise' education are discussed in the following pages. But each family is unique; each circumstance, each LEA attitude and approach different. So if 'statementing' is any sort of problem for you, learn as much as you can about the law and your LEA's own procedures, and *seek advice before you act.* The *Special education* *handbook** is indispensable. But if you need authoritative information you should refer to the Act and Regulations themselves.

If my child has special needs, can I educate him or her at home?

Yes. As amended by the 1981 Act, s 36 of the 1944 Act makes this clear:

> It shall be the duty of the parent ... to cause [the child] to receive efficient full-time education suitable to his age, ability, and aptitude, *and to any special educational needs he may have,* either by regular attendance at school or otherwise.

This gives the parent the right to educate *any* child 'otherwise'. (However, you need the LEA's consent to withdraw your child from a special school. See page 53.)

Can we 'opt out' of the statementing procedure?

Not necessarily. Most LEAs do issue a consent form when they notify parents that they propose to assess their child. But if they are determined to go ahead they will do so with or without consent; and if they ask you to present your child for examination, you are liable to prosecution if you fail to do so 'without reasonable excuse' (Schedule 9, para 5). Evidently this statutory provision overrides your general right to refuse permission for your child to be medically examined.

The LEA must assess your child if they think they will probably need to decide what special educational provision is required (1993 Act, s 167(2)(b)). Likewise they must make a statement if in the light of the assessment they still need to determine this provision. But one assumes they will not need to decide what provision is required if they will not be making it themselves. At any rate, it seems absurd for them to go ahead with statementing if you are determined to home educate. However, it is not always easy to convince an LEA of this fact, and you may need to consult others with experience of the problem in order to learn the best way to proceed.

*Available from Advisory Centre for Education (see page 125), price £7.50.

Our child has been/is being 'statemented'. Does this mean we lose the right to home educate?

No. Section 168(5) of the 1993 Act says that where an LEA maintain a statement they must arrange for the provision specified in it to be made *'unless the child's parent has made suitable arrangements'*.

'Suitable arrangements' refers to the duty of parents to secure the education of their children under s 36 of the 1944 Act (see page 63).

BE WARNED!

▸ Section 163 of the 1993 Act includes the words:

> Where a local education authority are satisfied that it would be inappropriate for the special educational provision … [called for] to be made in a school, they may arrange for the provision … to be made otherwise than in a school.

This section empowers *an LEA* to make 'otherwise' provision. But officers of several LEAs have tried to invoke it against parents who wish to home educate by saying it is *not* considered 'inappropriate' for the provision to be made in school. This shows a complete misunderstanding of the purpose of the section.

Part III of the 1993 Act may seem to impose on LEAs a duty to determine all aspects of a child's education, but a careful reading shows that this is not so. If your LEA try to tell you that s 163 has anything to do with *your* choice of home education, they are *wrong*. Your right to home educate as a parent is set out quite clearly in s 36 of the 1944 Act, as amended (page 63), and in s 168(5) of the 1993 Act (see above on this page).

▸ Parents are often told by LEA officers that they would need 'special needs training' in order to home educate a child with a disability or handicap. Of course this isn't true. In fact there are still many teachers, even in special schools, who do not have any formal 'special needs' training or qualifications.

A qualified teacher who chose home education for her handicapped child following a dispute with the authority over special or mainstream schooling was told she would only be 'given permission' if she allowed various home tutors, educational psychologists and other assorted 'experts' into her home to oversee and advise. This became too much when two of them began to come together, twice a week, and there was only one day of the week when no-one came!

A complaint on her behalf brought the response: 'Well, she admits she has no special needs training'! The LEA officer was promised that the matter could be discussed when the LEA could confirm that all of their teachers who taught 'special' children had special training - meanwhile the team of experts should be employed elsewhere!

Be confident!
You are the expert where your child is concerned.

Since the introduction of 'statementing', a growing number of parents have chosen to educate their 'special' children at home. They do not take this decision lightly or on impulse. Education out of school is a major commitment, whether or not a child has 'special needs'; but it can be a particularly daunting prospect for a parent whose child needs constant attention, or at an advanced age needs to be 'taken back to the beginning'.

However, our superior knowledge of our own children and our concern and care as parents provide a basis for a more effective education in many important ways. In particular:

- We can provide one-to-one teaching or interaction. For many 'special' children this is a *fundamental* requirement - but it is almost *never* available in schools.
- The home situation is inherently flexible - it is free from those administrative and physical constraints of the school environment which prevent the possibility of following the interests and motivations of the individual child.
- At home a child has time. More time to learn, more time to play, because less time is wasted on irrelevant activities (which are different for each child), and *no* time is wasted sitting on a bus. (For some children at rural special schools, travelling time can exceed three hours a day!)

Parents are in a better position to understand and cater for *all* aspects of their children's welfare. For example, many children have special dietary needs. Whilst failure to cater for these needs is not usually life threatening, it can often have serious consequences. Such children may need to avoid:

- eating too much *(- children with Down's syndrome, who often put on weight easily)*;
- eating too little *(- children with digestive abnormalities such as those caused by cystic fibrosis)*;
- eating foods which cause allergic reactions *(eczema, asthma, hyperactivity, behaviour disturbances)*.

Home educated children can have a better quality social life, because we are not obliged to impose artificial barriers (mainly of age and/or ability) to social contact. Our children can mix freely and confidently with people of varying ages and backgrounds - and this makes them more socially adaptable, outgoing and mature than their school-going counterparts.

This is particularly true for children with 'special educational needs', who are able to learn from real life - not separated into special schools; not marked out as different by the presence of extra helpers in mainstream schools - but truly integrated.

2.8 'Special educational needs' in Scotland

Scottish education authorities have a duty to identify children with 'pronounced, specific or complex special educational needs such as require continuing review'. To do this they must first carry out an *assessment*. If the assessment shows that the child's needs fit the above definition, they must then open a *record of needs* (1980 Act as amended, s 60-62).

In making an assessment the authority must obtain advice by means of:

- a medical examination (at which the parent has the right to be present);
- a psychological examination; and
- a report from one of the child's teachers.

If the authority want to assess your child, they must write and ask you to present the child for examination. When they do this they must:

- give you basic information about the assessment procedure;

The Scottish definition of *special educational needs* is identical in substance to the English one (page 60). It is given in s 1(5)(d)) of the Education (Scotland) Act 1980, which was itself added by s 3 of the Education (Scotland) Act 1981.

The Scottish law relating to special educational needs is set out in s 60-65G of the 1980 Act as substituted by s 4 of the 1981 Act and subsequently amended, together with the Education (Record of Needs) (Scotland) Regulations 1982.

- allow you at least three weeks to write back with your own views on the child's needs and how they should be met; and
- give you the name of an officer who can provide advice and further information.

(If you fail to present your child for examination without reasonable excuse, they must write again requiring you to do so. After that, you can be prosecuted if you still don't comply, but the authority's duty to carry out an assessment comes to an end.)

In deciding whether to open a record of needs, the education authority must consider not only the specialist advice obtained in the course of carrying out the assessment, but also any other relevant evidence, including your own views.

- They must then write and tell you straight away what they have decided and why.
- If they have decided to open a record, they must also send you a draft, giving you two weeks to comment on it.
- In drawing up the final document they must take your views into account.
- They must tell you what they decided to put into it.
- They must notify you of your right of appeal.

You can appeal against their decision to open a record as well as against its contents (s 63).

A record of needs must include:

1. an assessment profile;
2. a summary of the child's impairments;

3. a statement of the special educational needs arising from those impairments;
4. a statement of the measures the authority proposes to take to meet these needs; and
5. where appropriate, details of the school the child is to attend.

After at least a year you can write and ask the education authority to review

- their previous decision to open (or continue with) a record of special educational needs; and
- the information in the record.

The authority can also carry out a review without being asked, if and when they think fit.

We fully intend to educate our child at home. Is the education authority entitled to open a record of needs?

There is no clear answer to this question. The education authority have to 'record' any child with 'pronounced, specific or complex special educational needs such as require continuing review'. The child's record of needs then defines the special provision the authority must make.

If you are providing for your child's needs by other means, it seems pointless to go through the procedure of opening a record. You may be able to argue that the child's needs do not require 'continuing review' in this situation. But if the authority are determined to go ahead with the procedure, they may not be easily convinced by this argument. And in particular you are obliged to present your child for examination if asked.

If my child has been 'recorded', can I still educate him or her at home?

The law is not very explicit on this point, but with respect to 'school age' children, s 62(3) of the amended 1980 Act says:

> An education authority shall ensure that the provision made by them under this Act for a recorded child ... includes provision for his special educational needs.

This might be taken to imply that if the authority are not providing education for your child in the first place, they do *not* have to take the measures specified in the record of needs.

Can I withdraw my child from a special school in order to educate 'by other means'?

If you feel you can meet your child's needs more appropriately at home, there's no reason why you shouldn't consider doing so. However, to take your child out of *any* state school, you need the education authority's consent. (See page 59.)

2.9 Child benefit

Child benefit is paid for all children under sixteen and for some children over sixteen who are not yet nineteen. Once a child reaches sixteen, benefit is continued if they are receiving non-advanced full-time education by attendance at a recognised educational establishment. In addition, it *may* be paid for children being educated 'elsewhere', including those who 'could reasonably be expected to attend such an establishment'. In the latter case you must be able to show that such education was being provided immediately *before* the child reached the age of sixteen.

This 'elsewhere' provision was originally meant to cater for children with special needs, but the present wording, secured through pressure from home educators, specifically includes those who have opted for 'otherwise' education.

In order for benefit to continue, your education must be recognised by the Secretary of State for Social Security. In practice, presumably because they are not qualified to assess education, the Department of Social Security

> The current child benefit law is Part IX of the Social Security Contributions and Benefits Act 1992. Section 142 deals with payment of benefit after age 16. The Act is supplemented by regulations, the main ones being the Child Benefit (General) Regulations 1976. Although these were made under an earlier act, they are still in force at the time of publication.

(DSS) usually delegate this task to the LEA. When your child is fifteen the DSS send you a form to complete in order to declare whether (s)he intends to continue in full-time education beyond sixteen. If you indicate that you are educating 'otherwise' the Child Benefit Office in Newcastle is likely to ask your LEA to confirm that you are home educating satisfactorily.

Since most education at this age is exam oriented, it may be difficult to satisfy the DSS unless your child is studying for three 'A' levels. Sometimes a junior official will make an arbitrary decision, e.g., that one 'A' level plus work on an art portfolio is only part-time education and therefore not eligible for benefit. It may be even more difficult to help them understand that autonomous education is valid. One argument here could be that the LEA have been satisfied until now - otherwise they would have taken steps towards a school attendance order (page 49) - and they cannot become dissatisfied without a substantial reason. Considerable letter-writing may be necessary. Always re-read what you have written. How would it sound to a reasonable person? What impression would it make on a tribunal?

If your child is not continuing with home education you may still be entitled to child benefit between their sixteenth birthday and, for example, the start of YTS. Again it's worth persisting with letter-writing. It's also worth checking the regulations yourself in a good reference library. (Try compendiums of social security legislation.)

> In any claim for child benefit, if the DSS adjudicate against you, you can appeal to a tribunal.

2.10 The law in the Republic of Ireland

The Irish Constitution refers to education in article 42. This article reads (in part) as follows:

> 1. The State acknowledges that the primary and natural educator of the child is the Family and guarantees to respect the inalienable right and duty of parents to provide, according to their means, for the religious and moral, intellectual, physical and social education of their children.
>
> 2. Parents shall be free to provide this education in their homes or in private schools or in schools recognised or established by the State.
>
> 3. 1. The State shall not oblige parents in violation of their conscience and lawful preference to send their children to schools established by the State, or to any particular type of school designated by the State.
>
> 2. The State shall, however, as guardian of the common good, require in view of actual conditions that the children receive a certain minimum education, moral, intellectual and social.

The duty of parents is set out in s 4(1) of the School Attendance Act 1926:

> The parent of every child to whom this Act applies shall, unless there is a reasonable excuse for not so doing, cause the child to attend a national or other suitable school on every day on which such school is open for secular instruction and for such time on every such day as shall be prescribed or sanctioned by the Minister in respect of such day.

At first sight this seems to contradict art. 42(2) of the Constitution by excluding the possibility of home-based education. However, the right to home educate is contained in s 4(2), which gives a list of 'reasonable excuses', including (s 4(2)(b)):

> that the child is receiving suitable elementary education in some manner other than by attending a national or other suitable school.

Suitable education is not defined here. Indeed, although the Constitution (art. 42(3)(2), quoted above) refers to 'a certain minimum education', such a minimum standard has never been laid down in any subsequent legislation. This has led at least one commentator to the view that no court can lawfully conclude that any child is not receiving education of such a standard![*]

The expression 'child to whom this Act applies' refers to the child's age. Currently education is compulsory in the Irish Republic from the age of six until the child reaches fifteen, but for this purpose a child is not considered to reach any age until the first of four fixed dates following their actual birthday. These dates are March 31, June 30, September 30 and December 31.

Apart from home-based education, the other possible 'reasonable excuses' for not sending your child to school are:

- The child is ill.
- Any school to which you have no religious objection is too far away, and no suitable transport is available.
- There is some other 'sufficient cause'.

As a parent you have no legal duty to tell the authorities if you want to educate your child at home; but you can be served with a notice to provide information about any of your children, including their names and ages, and, if appropriate, details of how they are being educated (s 20). Quite apart from this, you can be served with a formal warning if you seem to have no valid reason for not sending your child to school (s 17). This gives you a week either to send the child or to provide a reasonable excuse. If you don't comply, you will be taken to court; and if you are found guilty and offend again within three months you can be prosecuted without warning. In court the onus is on you to show that the child was being suitably educated or that you had some other reasonable excuse (s 18(2)).

If you move to a new school attendance area, you have to inform the authorities in both the old and new areas within a week (s 6). Presumably this applies regardless of whether your child is being educated at school or at home.

[*]Brian Doolan, *Constitutional law and constitutional rights in Ireland,* 1984.

3

Your relationship with the local education authority

So you've decided home-based education is best for your child. You've thought about it carefully and you feel you can do it. If your child has never been to school (or perhaps if you've just moved to another area), there's no reason why you should necessarily have any dealings with your LEA at all. But if you're withdrawing your child from school, they will almost certainly want to know about your arrangements. And in any case you should be prepared for possible contact with them sooner or later.

In part 2 we considered the legal status of home education. Here we turn to the practicalities of your relationship with the LEA.

3.1 Dealing with the LEA

Although some LEAs are more positive than others towards home-based education, the vast majority are fairly cooperative and should be approached on that assumption. But an LEA is not necessarily monolithic, and in many cases it would be misleading to describe the authority as a whole as either good or bad. Sometimes they are divided into districts, and these can vary considerably. But in any case a lot will depend on the attitudes of the individual officers you have to deal with.

Most LEA officers will be trained teachers with some years' classroom experience who have chosen to move on to administration. Like many professional people they tend to believe in the system they work in and the structured approach that it involves, and they may feel threatened by what they see as anarchic deviations from it. They may privately be quite critical of the education authority they work for, of many of its attitudes, and indeed of the system as a whole; but if they see it attacked or dismissed by people outside their profession, they may see this as a threat not just to their profession but to themselves personally. Their role as teachers has convinced them, rightly or wrongly, that most of the problems among the young derive from bad home backgrounds or from social problems rather than from bad schooling: they may see schools as a haven of security and sanity for the young. Most of their experience of 'truancy' confirms this, and they may never have met the kind of solicitous family that withdraws its child from school from a genuine concern for the child's welfare.

Individual LEA officers often have widely differing views on the merits of home-based education. Some may have had no previous experience of it, and you could need to be patient while they acclimatise themselves. If you start from the assumption that their main concern is for the welfare of the children, you may be able to lead them to an understanding of your own perceptions of what your child needs. Other officers are highly prejudiced and will do their best to stop you educating 'otherwise'. If you are faced with an implacably hostile individual, you may need to ask the LEA to assign someone else to you instead. If you are an EO member the support of your local coordinator could be helpful here. Such prejudice rarely extends to the most senior positions in an LEA, but in the handful of authorities where it does, you could have to take further measures (see page 111). But many LEA officers are sympathetic to home-based education, and a few are even EO members. The Association now gets frequent enquiries from parents who have been referred to it by LEAs.

This variation in individual attitudes can sometimes lead to discrepancies in communication. Perhaps to your relief a visit or interview has gone particularly well, and you have been left with the impression that the LEA approve of what you are doing. Then a few days later you get a dictatorial and uncompromising letter, or a particularly damning report. Possibly the

The **Director of Education** (sometimes known by other titles including **Chief Education Officer** and, where appropriate, **County Education Officer**) is responsible to the council's education committee for seeing that general policy is carried out. (S)he may determine the prevailing attitude towards education otherwise than at school, but is unlikely to deal with individual cases in person unless they become serious public issues.

Inspectors or **advisers** (sometimes spelt **advisors**) are the officials you are most likely to have to deal with. There's no significance in the difference between these two titles. Inspectors/advisers may sometimes be prepared to offer you advice, but whatever they are called, their main function is to check that you are providing proper education. In at least one LEA they are actually told not to 'waste time' advising home educators. Some of them deal with particular subjects, such as English or maths, but those dealing with home educating families are more likely to specialise simply in either primary or secondary education (or occasionally, for want of anyone more appropriate, in special needs). Each inspector/adviser is responsible to one of the more senior administrators in the LEA. (Inspectors should not be confused with Her Majesty's Inspectors (HMIs), who are concerned with the inspection and recognition of schools.)

LEA officer felt unable to be forthright to your face. But it's just as likely that pressure has been applied in the meantime by others at the LEA. This is where it can be useful if you took notes at the time (see page 107).

Don't assume that all LEA officers are necessarily more conventional than you are. Some of them may be, but equally, others may be radical and idealistic. Don't distort the education you are offering in order to satisfy what you imagine are their preferences. Some LEAs have been quite disappointed at how 'boringly orthodox' their home educators are. A good LEA officer will delight in unconventional, creative children, and respect the environment which produced them.

In any contact with your LEA, make sure you're well informed of your rights and duties and can show you know what you're talking about. Avoid being either submissive or aggressive, but try to be civil, courteous, honest and reasonable at all times, even if you aren't always treated in the same way. If conflict should ever arise it will be useful if you can show you haven't put a foot wrong! Never allow mis-statements to go unchallenged, and don't respond emotionally to threats. Show that although you are prepared to be friendly and cooperative, you are also quite

Education Social Workers (ESWs), known in some areas as **Education Welfare Officers (EWOs)**, are experienced mainly in dealing with truancy and are not usually professionally qualified in education. If you've withdrawn your child from school in order to educate 'otherwise', it's important in any dealings with them to make sure they understand and accept the situation. If you have doubts about them or find them unhelpful, it may be better to establish links with your adviser. But ESWs are increasingly taking over the adviser's role with respect to home-based education in many areas, and if they've been specifically assigned to the job you may find it quite acceptable (see page 100).

determined to be firm. But don't seek unnecessary confrontation: try not to threaten the professional role of LEA officers, and avoid putting them in a position where they can't climb down without losing face.

When you communicate with the LEA, bear in mind that you're dealing with a collection of individuals, not a single entity. Many apparent problems are simply the result of ineffective communication, and you may be able to help with this. Don't assume the authority know something just because you've told one person by word of mouth - it's usually a good idea to confirm what you've said in writing (see page 108).

You may find all this advice bewildering and to some extent contradictory. If you've joined EO it could help to enlist the support of other members. Get in touch with your local coordinator, find out what you can about the LEA's usual attitude, and see if you can track down local members in a similar situation to yours.

Although it's advisable to be cautious and well prepared, there's every reason to be optimistic about your relationship with the LEA. However efficient or officious they may seem to be, LEA officers are just people. Some home educating families get on really well with them, and you may find you can establish some sort of personal relationship beyond the official one. And all the time, as more families take up home-based education the path is smoothed for others to take the same course:

> ▸ Dealing with the authorities has been a very empowering experience. You soon realise they're only human. Some are friendly and want to help; others aren't, but if we're calm and rational we can handle them. Helping other people with this has been very rewarding - you see them blossom in the same way. And you find you can apply what you learn

to other areas of your life too. As for the children, they see how much care we are taking to provide them with the freedom and resources they want. They learn you can live life the way you want if you tackle the problem rationally, whether you're dealing with your own parents or the outside world.

Finding out about your own LEA

If you want to know, for instance, the name and title of the chief officer, or the position of someone you have been in contact with, it's reasonable to ask the LEA for this without feeling obliged to explain why. Alternatively, the public library may hold information about its own authority. Two general sources of information which should be available at reference libraries are *Education year book* and *Education authorities directory*. These give details of all LEAs (plus a number of other things, such as examining boards), including the names of current holders of senior posts.

We believe our suggestions are sound, but we cannot accept responsibility for any disadvantage you may suffer as a result of carrying them out. We hope you find this publication helpful; but in the end you must exercise your own judgement in your relations with the authorities.

3.2 More about taking your child out of school

When can I do it?

It's helpful to wait until the end of term, preferably the summer one. You can then start trying home education at your own pace and without any pressure, since you won't have to commit yourself to it until shortly before the start of the next term. In the meantime you'll have had the chance to establish that your child really wants to learn at home, to see how it works out for your family, and to acquire some confidence in your arrangements. But if there's a crisis you may be forced to take your child out in the middle of a term. In this case it's important to avoid any suggestion of truancy by making your intentions clear as soon as you begin to home educate.

Who should I write to?

You'll need to write letters to establish that you're officially home educating. If you live in England or Wales it's essential to write to the head of the school to get your child's name taken off the register (see page 52). If your relationship with the school has been friendly, you may wish to give the reasons for your decision, but otherwise your letter can be quite brief and formal.

Specimen brief letter to headteacher

Dear Mr Taylor

Catherine Jones, 30.5.84

After careful consideration we have decided to withdraw our daughter Catherine from school in order to take personal responsibility for her education. Please could you delete her name from the admission register in accordance with Education (Pupil Registration) Regulation 9(1)(c), as she is now receiving education otherwise than at school.

We are grateful for all your help during Catherine's period at school.

Yours sincerely

Helen Jones
Malcolm R. Jones

Should you write to the LEA as well? It depends how confident you feel about presenting your plans. The head must tell the LEA in any case, but it could still be to your advantage to make the first move. Drafting a good statement will be hard work, but you should bear in mind that it will form the basis of a file on your child, which will then contain exactly what you want to say. If you are prepared to write about your intentions at some length, you may find the LEA are happy to accept them and take little or no further action. Even a brief letter may be useful, though, if it shows you are serious about what you are doing.

Specimen long letter to LEA

Mr R. Clark, Director of Education
Barsetshire County Council

Dear Sir

Michael Roberts, 18.12.91

We write to inform you that we are now taking personal responsibility for the education of our son Michael, aged 5½ years, otherwise than by attendance at school. We are doing this in accordance with our rights and duties as parents under section 36 of the Education Act 1944. We have written to his headmistress, Mrs Davidson, asking her to delete his name from the admission register under Education (Pupil Registration) Regulation 9(1)(c).

Michael has attended Greenhill First School for one year, but despite considerable help from Mrs Davidson he has failed to settle. He is normally a sociable, non-aggressive child, very self-willed but nevertheless amenable to reason, and pleasant to have around. He could read before he went to school, and enjoyed doing many things with us. Since going to school he has regressed in many ways and progressed in none. During the year he was very unhappy, had headaches and vomiting, bit his nails, was frequently slightly incontinent, insisted on being fed (something which he would never previously have allowed), had tantrums, refused to accept any checks or limitations when crossed - so that he had to be restrained physically - and, whilst often wanting to be cuddled, tended to react aggressively when his request was satisfied.

In school he was even worse. In the reception class he did not get on well with his teacher, but was at least happy with the other children, amongst whom he has made some good friends.

After the Easter holiday he was moved to a second year class, where he was bullied and became wildly aggressive himself. He still refused to conform to classroom requirements and was frequently disruptive. At the end of the summer term he was almost unmanageable at home and in school.

As the school holidays have passed, he has improved daily, and the change in his behaviour has led us to the view that it would not be in his best interests to return to school at present. When we asked him if he would like to learn at home instead, he was delighted and relieved, and is already almost his old self.

We have been keeping a diary to show what he does on his own and what his social life is like. We are aware of the importance of seeing that he meets his friends often enough, as well as mixing with people of all ages. We have joined a couple of groups with this in mind. When he is six he will have the chance of joining the Woodcraft Folk and possibly the local school of music, if he wishes. We know of a gym club, which he does not wish to attend at the moment. He has recently begun to enjoy swimming with friends, but has refused lessons.

Academically we are confident that in a one-to-one situation we can encourage the effective development of his abilities and aptitudes. We propose to use TV and radio programmes to catalyse interests and ideas in a number of areas. Reading is no problem: he does it all the time. On the other hand his writing is still hardly legible, and he resists doing it. Where learning can be achieved orally we intend to avoid contaminating its enjoyment with unnecessary written work. However, we aim to provide enough situations where writing is obviously necessary - and to keep it fun! He is very interested in maths and logic, and we see no difficulty in providing for this area of his development by various means - including the use of a computer where appropriate.

We have made plans for other activities: physical activity - regular visits to parks and playgrounds, yoga, cycling, swimming; music - listening, singing, playing instruments (sopranino recorder, glockenspiel, percussion); art - plentiful supply of materials, but we would like to know of an inspiring teacher for occasional 'art days', to help overcome our inhibitions; science - plenty of books with ideas; craft - he has his own workbench and likes making things; outings - visits to museums, etc.

On the basis of Michael's experience to date we feel that his social, academic and physical development are all best provided for outside the context of the school. We trust that you will respect our decision.

Please let us know if you would like us to provide any further information.

Yours faithfully

Alan Roberts
Caroline Roberts

◄ *This letter could easily be shortened by giving fewer details. For some general suggestions on correspondence with LEAs, see page 108.*

But you may be unsure of your plans at this stage, or you may feel uncomfortable about putting them into writing. Writing to the LEA is not essential, but if you don't volunteer any information they will have to take the initiative in seeking it. It could then be largely a matter of responding to their questions. All the same, you will still need to show them you have thought about what you are doing carefully. If you prefer to talk, you might want to propose a discussion, but in some LEAs you should be prepared for possible pressure to send your child back to school.

Are you taking your child out of a private school? If you write to say you're home educating, the head has to tell the LEA. If you don't, (s)he simply has to take the child's name off the register. But this may not be a very important distinction, as the head will probably ask which school the child is going to in order to forward the records. If your intentions aren't clear (s)he may well notify the LEA in any case.

What if I live in Scotland?

To withdraw your child from a Scottish state school you need the education authority's consent; but in the meantime it could count as an 'excuse' for absence from school if you are providing adequate education by other means (see page 60). If you can start during a holiday this should make things easier: hopefully your arrangements will be working well by the time you need to approach the authority.

To avoid any misunderstanding it's advisable to write to both the education authority and the school. Your letter to the school can be fairly brief, but the one to the authority will need more thought. If possible you have to convince them that your arrangements are sound and that an elaborate investigation is not necessary.

Mr K. Fraser, Director of Education
Mid-Albion Region

Dear Sir

Alison Graham, 4.3.82

We write to inform you that in accordance with our rights and duties under section 30 of the Education (Scotland) Act 1980, we are now taking personal responsibility for the education of our daughter Alison by means other than attendance at school.

Alison is 14 years old, and has been a pupil at Kirkwood High School, Muirbank, for three years. During this period...

[Continue with details of background to decision]

After giving the matter considerable thought we reached the view that our daughter's interests would be well served through education otherwise than by means of school. Over the course of the summer...

[Follow this with a general description of your arrangements]

We have now been engaged in home-based learning for several weeks. Alison is responding with enthusiasm, and we are confident that our provision is suitable to her needs.

We trust that you will respect our decision to take this step. We have written to Mr Mackenzie, the head teacher, to tell him of our intentions. Please let us know if you would like us to provide any further information.

Yours faithfully

John Graham
Fiona Graham

```
Dear Mr Mackenzie

                              Alison Graham, 4.3.82

After careful consideration we have decided to stop sending our daughter
Alison to school. We are now taking personal responsibility for her
education in accordance with our legal rights as parents. Please could
you therefore remove her name from the register.

We are grateful for all your help during Alison's period at school.

We have written to the Director of Education to explain our intentions.

Yours sincerely

John Graham
Fiona Graham
```

What will happen next?

Normally you can expect the LEA to contact you fairly soon in order to get more information. They may write or phone inviting you to come and discuss your arrangements with them; they may send someone to call on you; or they may simply send you a form to fill in. Even if no-one comes to see you straight away, most LEAs will propose a home visit once you have had a reasonable time to start home educating. All these situations are discussed in the following sections.

Often you will be sent some kind of information pack. Many LEAs have produced guidance notes for prospective home educators. These can vary considerably in tone, quality and accuracy. The best ones are friendly and positive; the worst can sometimes be intimidating and misleading. In either case they may not always reflect the approach of the people you will actually have to deal with.

Although LEAs have become more used to home education over recent years, it's still an exceptional situation for most of them. Sometimes there will be confusion and misinformation to start with:

> ▸ I wrote the standard letter to the headmaster, to arrive on the first day of the new term, and a letter to the Chief Education Officer with a copy of the head's letter. I also decided to take the bull by the horns and wrote to the advisers enclosing copies of both letters and asking for an

appointment to discuss same. I heard nothing from the advisers but got a phone call from the headmaster asking for James's new school so that he could pass on his records. I was taken unawares and said it wouldn't be necessary as I had informed the LEA. He was persistent, so I told him James was being educated privately at home. As a result of this conversation, the welfare officer arrived at the front door. (I asked him in, thinking he was someone I was expecting for an estimate.) He asked why I'd not been sending James to school. I went and got my notes, of which there must have been a dozen pages. I told him of my complaints about the teacher and the school and the system. He said I should consider another school before it went too far. I said I would like to see an adviser. He asked if I was a qualified teacher and said that I had to be approved by the Ministry of Science in London. He said what I was doing was against the law and I would find myself with an attendance order slapped on me. I was writing down what he said. Then I quoted the relevant Acts, etc., at him, and asked where he got his facts from. He started hedging and said I was making it difficult for him as I obviously knew the laws and he was wary of saying anything if I was going to write it down and possibly quote him. He said his concern was welfare not the law, but that I was getting myself into deep water although he appreciated my intentions were good. I said I wanted to see an adviser again, so he said he would arrange it as he couldn't stop me if I asked, but he would like me to try another school.

I didn't hear any further until almost the end of that term, during which time I had been extremely conscious of getting school-type work as evidence. Then one day the friendly neighbourhood welfare officer appeared again with James's attendance record from school marked absent all term. I said why had his name not been removed from the register as I had requested, and was a little more assertive this time. He said he didn't know why the advisers had not been, and what work was I doing with James. I said I would be pleased to show him if he could make an appointment, as it would take about two hours and I was about to go out. He said well it wasn't really his job and he would get an adviser to call.

Obviously, with all this, I was expecting the worst. The adviser phoned to come the week after the end of term. I had all the work laid out ready and all my notes. I had even kept a diary with every single thing we did each day. I contemplated taping our conversation but didn't go through with that. When she arrived she was the exact opposite of the welfare officer. She agreed with a lot of my complaints. She offered helpful suggestions. No question of allowing me to go ahead, it was a fact and she was here as an adviser, not an examiner. She even said that on a one-to-one basis we needn't do as much paperwork. She asked if it said how often she should come in any EO literature, but she said she would come once a term. I've not heard from her this term and there are only two days to go. But after I'd met her there was a weight lifted off me that I'd no idea I'd been carrying around for so long. I am still a little conscious of feeling that I've got to keep parallel to school work to some extent, which I hope will pass in time.

What if my child needs time to recover?

It may be hard to explain your arrangements to the LEA if you feel your child needs time to recuperate after problems at school (see page 15). A few LEAs may demand, 'Is this child school phobic or not? Take the child to a specialist. If labelled, (s)he's excused; if not, we require a full quota of work.' But the situation can rarely be defined as black or white in such a crude way.

Sometimes the only written work the child will do is about how awful school was. An inventive family can find endless essay titles on this theme. This provides evidence for the LEA that the child can write and is working, but is in no state to be pressured. It also provides a healthy outlet for the child, and the possibility of further talking and comforting.

Art, music and creative writing can be very healing. So can cooking, gardening, caring for animals and making things. Swimming, dancing and all kinds of large body movements may also have a place. This is not a conventional list of school subjects, but the more difficulties your child has, the more resourceful you may need to be in justifying your programme. You need to be able to show that what your child is doing is appropriate to his or her current abilities and aptitudes. (Avoid using the word 'needs', as you could unintentionally imply that your child has a disability, and this could give rise to complications - see pages 61 and 66.)

3.3 Providing evidence of education

Some LEAs are more demanding than others. Many merely wish to reassure themselves that you are sane and reasonable and are attempting to provide some kind of coherent education rather than neglecting your children or making use of their labour. Others may take a much closer interest in your arrangements. Often they may make specific demands, either by word of mouth or in writing.

As a parent you must see that your child is properly educated, and the LEA may ask you to show that you are doing this. Any more specific demand it may make is unlikely in itself to have the force of law (see pages 45 and 111). Sometimes you may have no difficulty in complying; but if you aren't happy the LEA is not entitled to insist. Your best course is to treat such demands as suggestions only. If you don't like them, you should explain why and propose a constructive alternative.

Probably the least controversial thing an LEA can do is to ask for a home visit (see page 97). Generally speaking these are a mutually convenient way of showing that education is taking place. But it would be unreasonable for an LEA to *insist* on a home visit (see page 103). So long as you have a good reason you can just as well seek to give evidence of education by some other means - such as a written report, for example. Conversely, if you are asked for a written statement of your aims you may prefer in the first place to suggest a discussion. The main thing is to keep a productive dialogue going without being unduly obstructive.

Negotiations with the LEA may be prolonged - this account covers over a year. Most LEAs would be less demanding for such a young child:

> ▸ It is now some years since we decided not to send John to school. He was due to start in January 1980 and would be five in the following February. As we had previously registered him with the village school, we notified the headmaster just before Christmas, and he in turn notified the Education Department. My husband and I were summoned to see the senior Area Education Officer and the Primary Schools Adviser. The atmosphere was quite pleasant and we were asked about our aims, our competence, and how we would deal with the social problems of isolation and the inevitable team sports. We were asked to supply a curriculum in writing and we said we preferred not to, but would send in something explaining our aims. This we did by February. It explained how we wished to follow John's interests in subject matter. We stated that he already read well and was moving quickly towards numeracy. We stated in general terms what we felt was important, i.e. an

understanding of the world we live in, etc. The Primary Adviser replied in writing saying that she was concerned at

> the absence of any reference to imposed discipline ... Society as we know it, whether acceptable or not, does demand whether we like it or not both self-discipline and submission to externally imposed discipline. The development of 'stickability' despite one's inclinations is a necessary discipline of learning.

She wished for more details and recommended some books, including one on pre-reading skills, even though I had assured her he read well. She suggested we experiment for one term and then submit a new expanded curriculum.

In June we replied reiterating that we were working in an individual-centred system designed to encourage choice, and obviously too rigid a curriculum was impossible. We then went on to list his achievements up to that point under various headings, also a list of visits of interest since January.

This was acknowledged with a wish that we contact her in December to show her samples of John's work so that she could assess the progress he was making. On my phoning for this appointment she suggested that I bring along notes on my plans for the next few months.

The meeting took place a fortnight ago and I attended with trepidation. I was not using any maths textbook or scheme, and much of my evidence of John's development I felt was in terms of conversations we had had together. I need not have worried. On the maths side (and I must confess here that I used to teach secondary level mathematics) she was pleased that I wasn't using a textbook. She said that most parents teaching their own children ploughed through a textbook because they thought it was what they would be doing at school, but that understanding in real life situations was much better at this stage.

We also discussed at length how having relaxed into the situation of home education I felt it less necessary to manufacture situations for learning, but was able to use my son's interests. It really does just happen if you are receptive to their ideas. Also use of suitable games gives practice in arithmetic and logical manipulation without drudgery. All this she accepted and tended to agree with, although she still wishes work discipline to be there.

At the end of looking through the samples of his work she mentioned the plan for the next few months. I said that I hadn't written anything down as I wished to discuss it with her. My aim was to continue with the sort of things we had done so far, widening our interests and following John's interests more. This she accepted and suggested I phone her at the end of the summer for a chat and to see how things are going.

It's a good feeling now that I am not committed to anything specific except to make progress - which is my hope for my son's education anyway. I feel that we are being treated as reasonable and responsible people, and certainly not being harassed.

About a week after this last meeting, the Primary Adviser was talking to a training course for playgroup supervisors and early education. She told them about a group of parents called Education Otherwise who were interested in their children's education from birth onwards, and the excellent work they were doing. This was reported back to me by a friend on the course, and was very reassuring - she may yet be joining us!

3.4 Timetables and curricula

Two items commonly requested by LEAs are a timetable and a statement of your curriculum. Obviously if you have them you can submit them, but many home educating parents are averse in principle to both, and they are not in themselves a legal requirement.

A certain daily routine may help one to organise time efficiently, but a *timetable* as usually understood in schools is an artificial device designed to solve a complex equation involving large numbers of children of mixed ages, a limited number of rooms, a range of staff skills and a particular curriculum. In a home, a timetable of this kind is likely to be a hindrance to the kind of flexibility that is one of the virtues of home-based education. For LEAs to insist on one is unreasonable.

One family who were asked for a timetable wrote back like this:

> Mr Fowler asks for details of time spent on various activities and suggests that a weekly timetable would be helpful. He states that our report gives a very clear picture of our view of education. We believe that our commitment to an autonomous approach is implicit in the report, but possibly we may not have made this perfectly plain. We consider that our role should be one of facilitating and responding rather than teaching and initiating, and for this reason we do not observe a preordained timetable.
>
> David spends most of the time he is awake on educational activities of one kind or another. We do not differentiate between term time and holidays. He does very little which could be considered to be

> time-wasting or non-educational, and since he does everything from choice he does not feel the need to take time off. Whilst he is not *made* to do any of the things listed by Mr Fowler it is clear from our report that in practice he does all of them, among others. We find that over the course of months the ground covered amounts to what could reasonably be called a conventional balanced curriculum. However, this is entirely a consequence of David's own interests, and we do not accept any external obligation to cover any specific subject. He is at liberty to specialise or diversify into other areas as his interests vary.
>
> We appreciate Mr Fowler's difficulties in categorising and quantifying our activities. We are unable to give details of time spent in specific fields of activity, although we do keep a day to day record as a basis for periodic reports. What we do not undertake to do is to log the actual hours spent on each of a fixed list of 'subjects'. We feel that this would tend to interfere with the normal course of our activities, and would in any case be likely to give a misleading picture in the short term.

A *curriculum* is more general in nature than a detailed timetable, and it may well be possible to devise one which is not too restricting. Although the dictionary defines 'curriculum' as a 'course of study' or 'range of subjects taught formally', the term is commonly used to refer to little more than a set of broad aims. (A *syllabus*, on the other hand, is a more detailed account of what will be taught in a particular subject.) No-one can say what a child will achieve, but only what they hope or intend the child to achieve. While schools, for instance, aim to provide children with certain knowledge or qualifications, only a small proportion of children actually achieve the 'higher' aims.

Most parents will want their children to work towards some general aims in the areas of language skills, mathematics, human studies, science, expressive arts, physical activity and craftwork. Education authorities are also often concerned about provision for social contact. There is likely to be more disagreement about the method by which aims are to be achieved than about the aims themselves.

At this level of generality, you may well find a written curriculum quite acceptable. After all, it is a convenient way of showing that you are 'imparting ... skills and learning by systematic instruction' (see page 44). But like the writer of the letter quoted above, you may not wish to commit yourself to a curriculum in advance because you feel that your child should determine the course of his or her own education. This is a perfectly tenable position (see page 92), so long as you are able and willing to explain it to the LEA.

If you allow your child to learn as (s)he wishes, you may choose to keep a detailed diary. You could use this to compile retrospective reports at intervals, which you could produce as an alternative to a statement of curriculum. At the same time they would enable you to keep track of the ground covered and identify any deficiencies in the resources and opportunities available:

> ▸ We always refuse to make any predictions, except very general statements to the effect that we are confident that Peter will become fully literate/numerate/independent/competent or whatever the point at issue is. We always write about what he *has* done, never about what he will do, or even what we expect or hope, which might imply some degree of pressure from us. Where we do compromise is in writing reports with conventional subject headings in mind, in an effort to help communications. We stress that he does not learn in a conventional way, and we accept no obligation to see that he studies the full breadth of the conventional curriculum - it is entirely his choice. But we find something to report on in each of the traditional areas, even if it is only to acknowledge that he has decided not to study this area for the time being and that e.g. we are satisfied that he has a good grounding in the subject, no blocks, and will be able to take it up again whenever he chooses. We try to second-guess what our inspectors are looking for, and to answer any educational anxieties before they ask, without raising others they hadn't thought of.
>
> We send a report before they visit, which makes the visit very relaxed - more of a social affair. We make cakes (home economics) and good coffee, and they sit back and give Peter an hour's undiluted attention, which he enjoys. They have really healed a lot of the damage his teachers did, and it's made me realise how seldom adults give children this amount of serious attention. They don't have to make notes, which pleases everyone. It's mostly our own words that go in our file - they only need to add a note of their own in confirmation.

> ▸ Our inspector asks families what their educational aims are. If they present themselves as conventional, he then demands the sort of things he would expect of a class teacher. If they have unconventional ideas, he acknowledges that under s 76 they have the right to choose what sort of education their children receive, but he expects them to be articulate about their ideas and able to defend them clearly.

EDUCATING ARCHIE

What is structure? Mrs G ponders....

The *national curriculum* is mandatory for state schools only (Education Reform Act 1988, s 1). Inevitably it has had an effect on the general educational climate, and to that extent it may influence the views of LEAs (and possibly courts of law) on what constitutes education. You may of course wish to take note of it if you are expecting your child to return to school at a later date. Nevertheless, any LEA officer who insists that you must follow it is mistaken.

What if the LEA insist that you should include particular elements in your curriculum, such as chemistry or organised games for instance? It would be difficult to show that any proper education can take place without some attempt to foster basic literacy and numeracy; but beyond that, all you need to do is offer your child a reasonably wide range of opportunities in keeping with his/her age, ability and aptitude (see page 44).

3.5 Autonomous education

Traditionally education is seen as the transmission of established knowledge, often equated with a range of school subjects. If you are happy with this view, you may feel you have no need to read this section.

But you may prefer to express your aims within a different framework, stressing the personal qualities and learning skills necessary to cope with an unpredictable future, and the role of self-direction in acquiring these qualities and skills. Views like this may be easy to grasp intuitively, but it's often harder to explain them to the LEA in an acceptable way.

If you believe your child should be allowed to determine the course of his or her own education, how can you justify this in terms of s 36 of the 1944 Act? One family argued as follows:

> Our provision is *efficient* because rather than force-feeding our child with information when she is in an unreceptive mood, we wait until she asks for it. As she is in control she is motivated to learn quickly and effectively without wasting time; and she is not just learning facts but is also learning how to learn. Our provision is *suitable* because she is free to move as fast or slowly as is right for her, to explore anything which particularly appeals to her as deeply and widely as she wishes, and to stop when she wishes. We offer further learning opportunities as appropriate in accordance with her responses.

(See also the letter on page 88 in connection with timetables and the duty to provide *full-time* education.)

Professor Roland Meighan, a longstanding member of Education Otherwise, is a leading sociologist of education with a special interest in the 'autonomous' model. He has prepared the following statement describing it as it might be applied to home-based education. If you have adopted a 'self-directed' approach, you may wish to adapt this statement to suit your own needs.*

> We have taken as our pattern the autonomous study ideology of education advocated by various leading educationalists, e.g. T. Husen in *The learning society* and L. C. Taylor in *Resources for learning*. The term *autonomous study* was adopted by the Council of Europe Committee for General and Technical Education in 1975 in preference to the expression 'independent study' or the term 'self-directed learning'. The emergence of autonomous study as the essential objective of European educational approaches is traced by the French educationalist V. Marbeau in *Education and culture* no. 31 of Autumn 1976, where he notes that the Berne Conference of European Ministers of State for Education acknowledged this approach in outlining the proposals for a diversity of learning and teaching methods to achieve a more individualised education and promote independent study by learners.
>
> The autonomous study approach is similar in key respects to that adopted in some UK schools, e.g. Summerhill and Dartington. Both these and other schools have been formally approved, and this approach is therefore legitimated in the UK as an alternative to the authoritarian-transmission ideology of most schools in the public sector. Confirmation of this was given in the judgment of Judge Roy Ward in the case of Harrison & Harrison v Stevenson in June 1981.†
>
> The characteristics of the autonomous approach may be described as follows:
>
> **Theory of knowledge - its content and structure**
>
> Knowledge may be interpreted as being predominantly past-orientated, present-orientated, or future-orientated. The first will rely on ancient subject divisions; the second on integrated attempts on the grounds that complex modern problems like pollution, terrorism, computer technology and mass media are both cross-disciplinary and in need of new information to cope with them; the third stresses the need for learners to concentrate on the acquisition of learning skills to cope with an uncertain

*For further discussion, see his book *A sociology of educating*, 2nd ed., Cassell, 1986.

†See page 44.

future and the personal confidence to use these skills in any circumstances in which they find themselves. The concept of the confidence-building curriculum of J. Hemming in *The betrayal of youth* is close to this third view.

The autonomous study approach adopts this third view, seeing subjects as useful secondary resources to this end and therefore an element in the learning programme rather than the dominant idea. Integrated studies are also seen as having a place because of their present-orientated nature, but again subordinate to the development of learning skills. Knowledge is seen as a network rather than as sequential or linear in structure.

Theory of learning and the learner's role

Learning may be viewed as a collective activity best organised in groups, or as predominantly an individual activity. It may be seen as a competitive activity, one learner against another, or as a cooperative activity, or as a personal development against criteria of achievement. Learning may be seen as low marks, censure and punishment, or as a necessary feature of human

EDUCATING ARCHIE

consciousness unless discouraged. Learning for some is seen as best achieved by listening, for others through visual means, by others through doing or active participation.

Self-directed learning is seen as the major approach in autonomous study and the stress is upon learning as an individual activity in the main, as a personal development against achievement criteria, as a necessary feature of human consciousness and achieved through active participation. The acceptance of some formal instruction and some textbook-based work is consistent with this approach, provided it is not the sole or dominant approach, and it is selected by the learner as appropriate to a particular task.

Theory of teaching

Teaching may be seen as the giving of instruction derived from a traditional subject, or as the organisation of learning situations, or as self-teaching through undertaking the organisation of learning situations oneself.

In the autonomous study approach, the self-teaching alternative is selected, supplemented by using other people as consultants and sometimes as instructors.

Theory of resources

Resources may be first, second or third hand experiences. An example of the last is a textbook that gives summaries of other people's ideas. Resources may be books, visual media or experiences in the environment. Access to resources may be direct or may be filtered through another, e.g. a teacher. The selection of resources tends to match the theory of knowledge and teaching so that past-orientated systems are likely to place heavy reliance on third hand experiences codified in textbooks and interpreted by a teacher.

In the case of autonomous study emphasis tends to fall on first hand experiences from the immediate environment and directly accessible to the learner. Second and third hand experiences are seen as useful supplementary resources.

Theory of assessment

The view of who is the appropriate person to undertake assessment varies. For some it is an external examiner, for others a teacher, for others the learners themselves. Assessment may focus on memorising information, skills, written end-products, or continuous assessment. It may take the form of tests, profiles, certificates or self-report monitoring. The purpose may be selective or diagnostic.

The appropriate pattern in the case of autonomous study would appear to be that of self-assessment, for diagnostic reasons, stressing skills both intellectual and physical. This does not rule out other forms of assessment, e.g. external examinations, if they are seen by the learner to be appropriate to a chosen purpose.

Theory of aims and objectives

The society for which education prepares learners may be envisaged in various ways. It may be seen as a perpetuation of society as it is, or some vision of a changed social structure. Some visions of the coming state of affairs stress a pluralistic society of considerable diversity and change, others an individualistic society with a dispersal of power, others a self-sufficient society with stress on small communities. All these visions that imply changes ahead require considerable flexibility and adaptability of young people.

Autonomous study adopts aims and outcomes related to a vision of society that requires flexibility, adaptability and self-reliance. This underpins all aspects of the educational programme. The success or failure of the programme is judged in terms of the degree to which the learner becomes self-reliant, personally confident, maintains intellectual curiosity and excitement, gains in mental agility and problem solving skills, uses first hand experiences and active participation in learning, is flexible, adaptable and self-critical.

3.6 Home visits

As a rule, a home visit is the most appropriate and effective way for an LEA to check that you are educating properly. Most authorities like to make them from time to time, and almost all home educating families are prepared to agree to them in normal circumstances. Although they are likely to face the first one with trepidation, their fears often prove groundless and the visit goes well - sometimes unexpectedly so:

> ▸ As Paula was five in December, I was expecting the dreaded visit from the LEA. Having spoken to the head of the LEA on a previous occasion, I was told I could expect a visit from the education officer, an education adviser, then a child psychologist. I don't mind admitting that on hearing all of this I was quite definitely quaking in my shoes. So I prepared myself for a fight if necessary.
>
> The longer I waited, the more I convinced myself I was going to have a hard time. However, I was determined to give a good impression: I kept the house neat and tidy - everything in its right place, the children well-groomed, and Paula's work neatly kept together. But then my mother became ill, my father came down with flu, so did the children, and lastly me.
>
> Then one miserable day, when the house looked like a demolition site, toys and washing in every corner, I felt like something the cat had dragged in, and we were each clutching firmly a handful of tissues and wearing big red noses, there was a knock at the door and there stood Mrs H - the education officer. I decided I had to make the best of a bad situation, and on inviting her in, cleared a space for her to sit down.
>
> 'So you're going to tackle it at home, are you?' she said. 'I don't blame you - I think it's a good idea.'
>
> Well!! After the mental build-up I had given her over the past few weeks, this was something I hadn't prepared myself for. We chatted for about an hour; she told me how sorry she felt for children at school who come out with a headful of knowledge that they will never use, and yet not properly prepared for life outside school. She said that in her opinion, Travellers' children who don't go to school are better educated for coping with life than those who do.
>
> I then brought up the subject of a timetable (which I understood the LEA would require). 'Oh no,' said Mrs H, 'I don't believe in them. It would be impossible to keep to a timetable at home anyway.'
>
> Well, what about Paula's social life then - I was sure she would require some explanation about this.
>
> 'But you have a social life, don't you? I'm sure you will see to it that Paula gets one too. There are very few children who are deprived of a social life. No, I'm not worried about that.'

ARCHIE INSPECTED
AND DO YOU FOLLOW A CURRICULUM?
LEA guide to EO
I TRY TO BUT THEY DON'T MAKE MUCH SENSE
WHAT ABOUT SOCIALISATION?
WELL THERE'S THE W.I. AND A NICE WOMAN NEXT DOOR
DO YOU USE THE TELEVISION?
YES, WE KEEP THE DOLLS HOUSE ON IT...
BUT WHAT ABOUT TAKING EXAMS?
I WON'T HAVE ANY TIME TO TAKE EXAMS SO LONG AS I'M TEACHING ARCHIE AT HOME
SEG

After looking at some of Paula's work she said, 'There would be no point in sending Paula to school just now anyway, as she is far more advanced than schoolchildren her age, and it would be a setback for her as she wouldn't learn anything new for some time yet.'

Lastly, having in mind the other visitors I had expected, I asked who would be calling next.

'No-one,' she said. 'I see no need for anyone else to come. I'm quite satisfied with what I've seen.' She then asked my permission to come sometime in the future to see how we are getting along, and I agreed.

It's good to know that some of *them* are on *our* side, isn't it?

The experience of another family is more typical:

▸ The day of the meeting arrived, and to our relief the Deputy Director arrived unaccompanied. We had envisaged that his concern would be the theory, whilst the adviser's would be practice. We'd decided that we would volunteer little of our radical ideas and convictions and try to stick to answering his questions. We felt that anyone rising to the post of Deputy Director would be sufficiently convinced in the system to resent our slamming it in his face. Over coffee in the kitchen this view was confirmed. The first of the two hours he stayed didn't go well - helped by our close-bosomed approach. So the time came to open things up a bit and explain the emotional considerations in not sending Nick to school, still steering more or less clear of the deschooling theory. The approach worked. It didn't take long to get across to him what he really wanted to know:

1. We were intelligent, sensible and sensitive parents who had our children's best interests at heart rather than solely our beliefs; and

2. We were capable and determined to provide for all our children's needs in the future, even where this meant exploring new ground ourselves.

Nick helped sway his last doubts by reading to him, his naturally achieved standard having shot several years ahead in the few months since leaving school. Though still unconvinced of our wisdom, the Deputy Director accepted our course of action with routine warnings about being on our own and not to expect help from the LEA. After which, to our delight, he left with a casual remark about sending an adviser to see us in a year's time.

These parents were unusual in being visited by anyone as eminent as a deputy director. An adviser would be more usual. But certain common features are worth noticing:

- The official was much more concerned with establishing that, in his terms, the parents were sane, intelligent and capable, than with studying what work the child had done or examining what schemes of work he was following.
- He was reassured by evidence of some competence in basic skills.
- He showed no desire to monitor the child's education closely.
- Though neither enthusiastic about nor supportive of home-based education, he was not obstructive.

Some LEA officials may themselves be confused about the legal position, giving the parents the opportunity to take the initiative:

> ▸ Mr Brown sat opposite us, clasping a bulky volume of *The law of education* with several markers inserted into the pages, and he started the conversation by inviting us to tell him a few details such as which school the children attended and their ages ... Mr Brown seemed reasonably happy about our overall presentation, saying that we had quite obviously given the problem a great deal of thought. He then referred to our original letter to him in which we had asked about deregistration, and told us that he wasn't at all sure what the correct procedure was. He couldn't say whether it was up to us as parents to deregister, or up to the education authority, but he would pass all the details of our interview on to the Director of Education if we were certain that we still wished to carry on with home education.

Usually LEAs send inspectors or advisers (see box on page 75). But because of cuts, government pressure and increasing numbers of home educators, some LEAs are becoming reluctant to provide advisers' time for home visits. Sometimes this has resulted in increasingly perfunctory and unhelpful visits from advisers; but other LEAs have dealt with the problem by assigning well-trained ESWs to the job of monitoring home educators. They are not qualified to inspect, and ESWs in this role may often be happy to assume that families are educating competently and conscientiously - they will only alert an adviser in case of doubt (in which case, if the family satisfy the adviser, all is well). The ESW will keep in touch, perhaps by an annual visit, perhaps only by a phone call to check that the children are still being home educated. If an ESW (or EWO) turns out to be misinformed or hostile, you may have to insist on being seen by an adviser; but if you are happy with the situation this is obviously unnecessary:

> ▸ An EWO turned up when I was in a foul mood. I'd heard of bad experiences with EWOs from several people. One woman had explained her educational philosophy for an hour to an EWO, who seemed sympathetic, but then as she went out of the door she remarked out of the blue, 'You do realise you'll be the one to go to court, not the child?' Another EWO had given a mother a formal warning of a school attendance order at the same time as a form 'to request permission to home educate'.
>
> I asked the EWO in and waited eagerly for her to put a foot wrong so that I could take her apart. Perhaps she realised - she behaved impeccably. She checked Michael's name and age and that we were still home educating him; then she asked if I'd mind if she said 'hello' to him. I called and asked him - he came, literally said only 'hello', and then sat and listened fascinated to the rest of our conversation.
>
> She told me our file had come through to her from our previous LEA (after 18 months) and quoted some of the nice things our previous inspectors had said. Then she named someone at the office and asked if we'd get in touch with him. I said we'd send him a report. I offered her a cuppa and she relaxed and spent the rest of the hour telling me horror stories about her job. She seemed impressed that the first thing I did when she came was to make a note of her name and position - said I was obviously competent, though that seemed flimsy evidence to me. We sent the report in, got an acknowledgement, and didn't hear any more for two and a half years, when we got a card from the EWO asking us to confirm that the position remained unchanged.

Home visits are normally arranged in advance. If someone arrives at your door unannounced, you should think carefully before letting them in. If you are alone or feeling unprepared it's quite reasonable to say that it's not convenient and that you will only accept visits made by appointment at mutually acceptable times. If they refuse, they are implying that their time is more valuable than yours. Keep a clipboard, paper and pen by the door, and take note of the name and position of callers and of anything significant they say. Be polite and pleasant but firm. Confirm your child's name and age and that you are home educating, and say that you will be pleased to discuss it further at a more suitable time (or that you will be happy to send a report). Remember that they have no right of access and don't let them pressure you into letting them in.

When you're expecting a visit it's a good idea to have someone else with you if you can. This could be a partner, a friend, or another EO member. If you don't feel confident, they will be able to provide support; they may also be useful as a witness if there should be any disagreement over what took place. It's reasonable for both parents to want to be involved in any discussions, and it should be possible to arrange an evening visit if necessary.

When an LEA officer has carried out a visit, you can assume that (s)he will make notes and that these will form the basis of a report. Some LEAs routinely send copies of such reports to the family; but unless there is a local policy of open government they are not obliged to do so. Whilst you have a statutory right (on written request) to see educational records kept by schools, this provision does not extend to reports of home visits made by LEAs.

If the LEA refuse you access to their reports, they are being unduly secretive. The situation should not be an adversarial one: both parties should be working together for the good of the child, and this aim is best achieved if everything is in the open. It is hard to see why any distinction should be made between school records and LEA records, and morally if not legally, you should be allowed to see what has been written about your arrangements.

Some parents have successfully insisted on being given a full copy of the LEA's report as a precondition for allowing a home visit (see page 106). An LEA may say, 'It is not our policy to ...' as if that makes something acceptable and unalterable. But they are the community's servants, and we should tell them when we require them to act differently. In one area several families cooperated in refusing visits until the LEA agreed to treat them as equal partners in the education of their children; but they were careful to provide alternative evidence of their education in the meantime.

There are no rules about the frequency of home visits. As LEAs become more experienced with home education they tend to feel less need to monitor it anxiously. Advisers' time is very expensive, and once they are satisfied with a family's arrangements they may well decide they are more usefully employed elsewhere. After this initial period few LEAs inspect more than annually. Some tag their files so as to pick up children at the start of secondary age, or at ages 7, 11 and 14. Others ask for occasional reports, and only visit if they do not find these adequate. One or two LEAs ask to visit much more frequently than this, perhaps once a term or even more. In one area this is a deliberate attempt to pressure the families to put their children into school. If you feel this is disrupting your arrangements or causing unnecessary stress, it's quite reasonable to ask for visits to be made less often.

So far in this section we have given a number of personal accounts of home visits from the parents' point of view. In conclusion, here are a few words spoken by an inspector:

> ▸ This is my first visit to a home educating family. I didn't know what to expect, and I had a certain amount of apprehension. But the other inspectors said, 'Oh, an EO visit. What fun - you'll enjoy that.'

3.7 Access and assessment

Most home educating parents are quite happy to let LEA officers see their children in the course of a home visit. But some choose not to, either to meet particular circumstances or as a general principle:

> ▸ No-one goes around checking every family to make sure their children aren't being ill-treated - they only step in if they have reason to think there may be a problem. Arguably child abuse is more serious than failure to educate, so why should LEAs have routine access to home educated children? This is why we decided we wouldn't let them see Gina. All the same, I'm very conscious of the responsibility the community has to ensure that its children aren't being abused. Plenty of other people had access to her, and she was running round the village playing with all the other kids.
>
> We also accepted that our decision meant that we had to put more effort into satisfying the LEA. We let them into the house and sat talking to them over coffee for hours, arguing points of law. They could hear Gina giggling outside the door and running past the window - she thought it was all hilarious. Eventually we had her independently assessed by a teacher and a social worker for maths, reading and social development. I wrote long screeds to the LEA over several years to explain what we were doing. We told them we considered visits to be unnecessary, but they still came back from time to time. We never allowed them access and eventually they stopped. We were very up-front about it - we had articles in the paper and were interviewed on

TV. In the end they were quite satisfied - they asked me to lecture at their in-service trainings.

But if they decide to refuse access, parents should be particularly careful to behave reasonably. As one EO coordinator writes:

▸ One family asked for help because the LEA were threatening to take them to court. They didn't want to allow access to their children, so we explained that this meant that they must work harder to satisfy the LEA in other ways. The parents came across as rather odd, and we were torn - we didn't want to be judgmental but we could see why the LEA were uneasy. It turned out that the parents hadn't answered any letters, hadn't answered the door, hadn't made any attempt to satisfy the LEA and still didn't do so after we had discussed it with them. When they asked for help, they meant money to fight the court case - they weren't prepared to give an inch. The children were taken into care and sent to boarding school. You've got to stand by what you believe in, but you've got to understand the LEA's position. If they can't get information they may get genuinely worried about a child. If we appreciate that, then we can take appropriate steps to satisfy them without letting them invade our lives.

Sometimes the issue of access can arise almost by accident:

▸ We didn't refuse access on principle - we'd been very happy with our previous inspectors. Then the LEA wanted to send a man who had behaved badly in another case - nothing to do with home education - and we said we wouldn't have him in our house or associating with our child. We said they could send someone else; but they wouldn't because that might imply that they accepted what we said about him.

A deputy director rang and tried to bully me. He blustered a lot - 'I'm sorry but you'll have to ...' - and I burst out laughing. It was a fortunate reaction, much better than losing my temper or being sarcastic. I said I was sorry we were making extra work for him personally, but he must know it was up to us to offer evidence to the LEA, and the choice of evidence lay with us. We would send in a report. 'What if we don't find your report satisfactory?' 'Well, we'll consider that if it arises, bearing in mind that you must be reasonable.' He rang off amicably and we sent in a detailed report.

We got a letter back from the inspector we wouldn't have, asking questions just to try and get us to write to him. We wrote back to the Deputy Director, who again asked us to communicate directly with the inspector. Some months later we received a letter threatening court action if we wouldn't allow a member of the advisory team to visit. We pointed out that we had always said we would welcome anyone except

Mr X, but we had no legal obligation to do so; and we enclosed another report. We had a casual word with our local councillor, who's on the education committee. We received a letter back thanking us profusely for our reports. It was four years before they sent an inspector.

The LEA may wish to satisfy itself that education is taking place by assessing the child in some way. For some parents this will pose no problem, but others may be very concerned about the form assessment takes. This again is a matter for negotiation. One parent who was concerned about assessment of her young children had this experience:

▸ The thing that concerned me most about the impending visit of the adviser was that it would undermine our children's confidence in our position as parents, which I feel is an innate need which children have: I didn't want them to feel that someone outside the family had more influence over their lives than us. I therefore gave a lot of thought beforehand as to how best to approach this with her, because I felt it most likely that this need in a child would not be one which she had considered. So at the earliest opportunity after she stepped in the door and the children were out of earshot, I put my point to her, prepared for the discourse to follow. To my utter amazement, and of course great relief, she not only immediately agreed with me but, I realised, actually understood and shared my viewpoint.

Even when children are older, many parents are firmly opposed - like John Holt* - to all forms of testing, arguing that it is degrading, inaccurate and misconceived. Parents may be particularly worried if their children have already had damaging experiences of schooling.

A compromise which has been used by a few parents is for assessment to be carried out by acceptable but professionally qualified adults - often friends or other EO members

Most EO parents allow the LEA access to their children but keep contact informal, drawing the line at any kind of formal testing:

▸ The LEA tried to insist on testing her on the grounds that they could not satisfy themselves as to whether the education provided was appropriate until they established scientifically what her ability and aptitudes were. We didn't get involved in discussions on the pros and cons of IQ tests. We just said it wasn't a legal requirement and we wouldn't allow it. We said we would only allow her to be assessed

*See for instance *Teach your own*, p. 205.

The only circumstance under which you are obliged to allow access is if the LEA ask to assess your child 'under Part III of the 1993 Act' (in Scotland, s 60-62 of the 1980 Act) or because they 'suspect (s)he has special educational needs' and are 'considering making a statement' (in Scotland, 'opening a record'). Under Schedule 9 to the Education Act 1993 you must present your child for medical, psychological or educational examination as required, and it is an offence not to do so without reasonable excuse. (A similar provision applies in Scotland.) If the LEA propose to assess your child under the 1993 Act, they must first give you four weeks' statutory notice with an explanation of the procedure and your rights. (In Scotland, three weeks, under the 1980 Act.) For further information about special needs, see page 60. (For Scotland, see page 66.)

> through informal discussion with one adviser who had established a friendly relationship with her, in the same way as a teacher does.

Sometimes, as in the following extract from a letter, it may be useful to insist explicitly on certain preconditions before allowing access:

> We are normally happy to receive visits from an adviser, as this seems a sensible and simple way of allowing the LEA to satisfy themselves. We would point out however that this is our own choice: there is no legal requirement for us to allow access to our child, and we are at liberty to offer you evidence of our educational provision in any reasonable way. We will only allow a visit on the following terms:
>
> 1. The visit is made at a mutually convenient time by a person acceptable to us, and the appointment is confirmed beforehand in writing, giving the name and position of the person who is to make the visit.
> 2. The person who visits us is committed to establishing a warm and friendly relationship with our child.
> 3. (S)he has read all our previous reports, and can show an open mind and some understanding of our philosophy of education.
> 4. As soon as practicable after the visit, we receive a full copy of his/her report.

Of course, in a good relationship with an LEA, these conditions will be observed as a matter of course. On the other hand, if problems should arise it may be an appropriate tactic to spell them out.

3.8 Taking notes

When you have a conversation with someone from the LEA, it's a good idea to make a note of when it happened, who you spoke to, and what was said. This applies both to phone calls and to meetings.

With phone calls it's a fairly simple matter. You can take notes with your free hand as the call progresses. Usually you will be told the name and position of the person you are talking to; but if you aren't, or if you don't hear it the first time, you can ask for this information without embarrassment. Don't forget to make a note of the date on which the conversation took place.

Most meetings and visits take place by prior appointment. You can normally expect to know in advance who you are going to see and when. There's no reason why you shouldn't take notes at the time as a matter of course, without any concealment. It's best to get in the habit of starting off formally, even if after a while the meeting gets so relaxed that you feel you can afford to put your clipboard down.

By taking notes you are doing three things. Firstly you are keeping a record of the proceedings. This could be quite useful if, for instance, you get a letter a few days later implying that something quite different happened. Secondly you are signalling to the other party that you are taking what they say seriously. This in itself often has a surprising effect on the nature of what is said. But if any statement seems unreasonable or improper, you can ask for it to be confirmed in writing. And failing that, you can read back your notes in order to check what was really meant. This too can be surprisingly effective, and you will often find that something entirely different is said the second time round. The third reason for taking notes is a very practical one: if you are nervous, holding a clipboard gives you something to do with your hands!

Occasionally people make tape recordings of conversations. For phone calls, an answerphone attachment could be useful if you can hit the record button during the course of an exchange. It's probably unnecessary to record a home visit unless you know there's likely to be serious conflict. There's no reason why you shouldn't tape what goes on in your own home, but it would be discourteous not to make it clear to your visitor that you were doing so.

On occasion LEA officials have been known to say things on the phone or in person which they wouldn't dream of committing to writing. Where there are problems, a transcript could be useful if you wish to make a complaint or to insist on having a less biased officer assigned to your case.

3.9 Writing to the LEA

Sooner or later you may need to write to the LEA. If you're skilled and experienced at writing business letters, this will not be too difficult. But many excellent home educators are less confident when it comes to writing to the authorities. If you're one of these, you may find these notes some help. And even if you write letters easily, you could find it useful to compare these suggestions with your own habits.

Who to write to

If you haven't already been in contact with anyone, it's normally best to address your communication to the Director of Education (or Chief Education Officer). You should be able to get their name, sex and official job title from the council offices or library, together with the address of the appropriate office. You can address your letter to them by name (followed by the name of their post), but as you aren't likely to be dealing with them in person, it's normally appropriate to begin the actual letter with 'Dear Sir' or 'Dear Madam' as the case may be.

If you've already had letters from the LEA, their stationery will probably make it clear who you're expected to write to. Often there's a convention that all correspondence should be addressed to the chief officer, but this doesn't mean they're likely to read your letter in person.

If you're answering a letter, you'll obviously be writing back to the person who sent it. But this isn't always as simple as it seems. Letters from junior LEA officers are sometimes signed by, or on behalf of, a more senior person even though (s)he may have no personal involvement with the correspondence. In this case write back to the senior officer, but don't forget to quote any reference given. This will generally include the initials of the person who actually gets to read your letter.

Alternatively, if you want your letter to reach a specific person you can mark it for their attention at the beginning of the address. If you particularly want the chief officer to read your letter, mark it 'for the personal attention of...'. But don't do this unless you have a good reason (e.g. a serious complaint against a subordinate).

What to say and how to say it

Occasionally you'll only need to write a sentence or two, perhaps to give the LEA a piece of information. In this case there should be no problem - the briefer you are the better. But most letters will be longer and more complicated than this, and usually there will be something you *want*, even if you're unclear at first about exactly what it is.

- Ask yourself what you're writing *for*. If your letter has no obvious purpose, the LEA will be unable to take it seriously.
- Avoid writing about two or more distinct problems in the same letter.
- Do one or two rough drafts first, until you get it right.
- Start by explaining what you're writing *about*. (Don't skimp on this, even if you think it's perfectly obvious.)
- Keep to the essential facts, presented in a logical order.
- Be as brief, clear and simple as you can.
- Don't be too formal or pompous.
- Keep your sentences short and avoid unnecessary long words - they look pretentious rather than educated.
- Avoid getting emotional.
- Resist the temptation to be sarcastic or witty.
- Remember to explain what you want.
- Read your draft through carefully. Take out everything that's unnecessary, and rewrite anything that's unclear.

Presentation and procedure

- If possible type your letter, so that it's absolutely clear what you've said. If you don't have access to a typewriter or word processing facility, be sure to write legibly and lay your letter out clearly. (Unlined notepaper is considered to give the best impression.) And if you do use word processing, keep it simple and resist the temptation to do anything too idiosyncratic with the layout.

- Remember to keep a copy. (If you have access to a photocopier, take a copy before posting. If you're using a computer, it may still be advisable to keep a copy of the final version on paper for extra security. Otherwise use good quality carbon paper. If all else fails it's better to keep a handwritten draft than nothing; but before you post the fair copy remember to correct the draft to take account of any further changes you made.)
- Don't forget the date, and make sure you also have it on your own copy.
- If you're answering a letter, quote any reference given.
- When writing about your child(ren) it's helpful to begin with a heading giving their name(s) and date(s) of birth.

...And finally, as well as keeping copies of your own letters, don't forget to keep any letters you get from the LEA. (See page 111.)

3.10 Keeping organised

Home education is not usually noted as a bureaucratic activity, but a minimal degree of organisation is an advantage, both for your own satisfaction and for the sake of your (ongoing or potential) relationship with the LEA. The problem has three aspects:

1. Your child's work
It would be a mistake to allow the obsessive collection of artefacts to interfere with the normal course of education. Nevertheless, it's wise to see that any written or graphic work is discreetly organised in such a way that it can be produced as evidence in case of need. Your child may take more or less responsibility for this, depending on age and temperament.

2. Records of your child's work
It's a good idea to try to keep a diary of your child's activities, however unlikely some of them may seem to be at the time. You wouldn't necessarily want to show it to the LEA - for one thing, they might not understand the peculiar rhythms of home-based education; but you might want to draw on it from

time to time to construct a more systematic account of what you and your child have been doing.

3. Communications with the LEA

Keep all letters, copies of letters, and notes of discussions and phone calls filed in chronological order. Have the file available during any visits so that you can refer to it if necessary.

3.11 Unreasonable demands and misleading communications

You should try to be reasonable in your dealings with the LEA. At the same time you have a right to be treated reasonably yourself. Many LEA officers are fair-minded and unprejudiced. But where bullying occurs the families most vulnerable to it tend to be those who are too diffident, too ready to compromise, and too willing to give way.

It's sometimes surprisingly easy to stand up to bullying:

▸ The very first communication we got from our LEA was a school attendance order. We wrote a long letter back, explaining exactly what we were doing and why. That was four years ago. Since then we haven't heard another word.

▸ Our lives were a constant nightmare for two years. We tried every method we could think of to get Marie to go to school. At the same time we were constantly pleading with the LEA to let us keep her out. But they were adamant that we would have to provide ten hours a week qualified tuition. Then we joined EO and found out that this wasn't necessary. I rang them up and said, 'I know my rights now. I'm taking her out.' All they said was, 'Put it in writing.' We did, and that was the last we heard of it.

If you think your LEA is treating you unreasonably there are various things you can do:

- If you are a member of EO you should first discuss the problem with your local coordinator and/or other experienced members.
- If necessary you can also contact the EO legal group.

- If there is a problem with a particular LEA officer, you may wish to write a letter for the personal attention of the Director of Education (or Chief Education Officer).
- If necessary you could write to the chief executive of the council.
- You could discuss the problem with the appropriate local councillor and/or a member of the education committee. (If you need your councillor's name and address you can get it from the council offices, the library, or a citizens' advice bureau.)
- If the problem has still not been resolved you could complain to the local ombudsman (see page 114)
- If legal action is in progress or has been threatened, it will usually be advisable to consult a solicitor (see page 118).

A few LEAs have forms asking for qualifications of the person teaching your child, the place where teaching will take place, and so on. These can be misleading, for instance by implying that it's illegal to educate 'otherwise' without a qualification (see page 45). Some routine LEA communications may even warn that you can be prosecuted under the 1993 Act for failing to educate. This is true, but it's rather like welcoming parents of reception class children with warnings of possible prosecution for truancy - and it's probably less likely to happen.

Some letters may ask you to reply within fourteen days. Often this stipulated time limit will have no statutory basis. But if the letter asks you to satisfy the LEA that you are educating properly, it could be the first step in the school attendance order procedure (see page 49).

Whatever the case, you should never ignore a letter. No matter how inappropriate the communication may seem, you should try to respond in some way within a reasonable time. You may need time to get some support before deciding what to do. If so, don't delay without giving an explanation. It's better to send a short but prompt reply by way of acknowledgement. For instance, you could write back to say that you aren't happy about the LEA's letter, but you're seeking advice before responding at greater length.

New home educators sometimes find it difficult to complain about negative attitudes, perhaps because they haven't yet developed confidence in what they are doing. One family moved to a new area after years of

Complaints to the Secretary of State

If your LEA behave unreasonably, you have the statutory right to make a complaint to the appropriate Secretary of State. In England, this is the Secretary of State for Education; in Wales and Scotland, the Secretary of State for the relevant jurisdiction.

Intervention by the Secretary of State is provided for in the 1944 Act (s 68 and s 99) and in the Scottish 1980 Act (s 70, for acts of omission only). The Secretary of State can only intervene if the LEA engage in 'conduct which no sensible authority acting with due appreciation of its responsibilities would have decided to adopt' (Secretary of State for Education and Science v Tameside Metropolitan Borough Council, 1977). Although the Secretary of State has intervened in favour of a home educating parent on at least one occasion, such cases are in fact extremely rare. In most situations other courses of action will be available, and they are usually more likely to be effective.

successful home education. In response to condescending letters from their new LEA they wrote:

> ▸ We have been home educating Sally and Sean for eight years, and we never received such patronising letters from our old LEA. We have always had a good and equal relationship with them, and expect the same courtesy from you. Are these letters specifically designed to discourage parents from exercising their rights? They must be perceived as intimidatory by new home educators. We suggest that you take steps to improve the situation, not just for us but for all home educators. We are considering complaining to the ombudsman, and will not accept any home visits until this matter is resolved to our satisfaction.

They sent a copy of this letter to their EO local coordinators, who had been collecting complaints about various LEA practices from other members. The coordinators wrote to the LEA listing all the complaints, and followed the letter with a visit to the education offices. At this meeting they found the LEA anxious to negotiate new procedures.

In EO we are working steadily to improve the standard of LEA communications. The DFEE take the view that rather than issue a circular it's better for EO to work with each LEA individually, giving them examples of good practice. In some areas this takes constant monitoring as new staff alter previously agreed standard letters - in one case the local coordinators have had to renegotiate three times with successive LEA officers in four years. But as EO becomes better known, LEAs are consulting the Association routinely in the course of revising their standard letters and policies with regard to 'otherwise' education.

3.12 The local ombudsman

If you think you have been unfairly treated by the LEA (or by any other department of the council), you can ask the local ombudsman to investigate (see page 126 for addresses). You are encouraged to go to your local councillor first, but you may wish to mention the local ombudsman from the start - it may encourage them to take you seriously. The councillor may want to try and deal with the problem him- or herself in the first place, but should be prepared to refer it to the local ombudsman if necessary. If you are in a hurry (for instance if you are threatened with a summons), or if your councillor is unhelpful, you can complain directly to the ombudsman without going to the councillor at all.

The local ombudsman investigates cases of injustice caused by maladministration. He or she will want to know:

- what the LEA did wrong or failed to do;
- what personal injustice you suffered as a result; and
- what you think they should do to put things right.

Among other things, maladministration can include:

- delay;
- failure to reply to letters;
- malice, bias or unfair discrimination;
- not telling you of your rights;
- not giving reasons when asked;
- failing to provide information;
- giving incorrect or misleading information or advice;
- not keeping promises;

- threats;
- rudeness or discourtesy;

and other similar kinds of unreasonableness. What the local ombudsman can't do is to intervene just because, for instance, you disagree with the LEA's opinion about the suitability of your educational arrangements. There has to be an element of maladministration. So it would be quite in order to complain that:

- you asked what alternatives there were for your school-refusing child, and were not told about home education

  (not telling you your rights; failure to provide information);
- you asked about home education and were told that the teachers were too busy to send work home, the LEA could not provide a home tutor, and if you did it yourself you would have to provide ten hours a week of qualified tuition

  (incorrect information);
- an EWO called and told you you would be taken to court if you continued to home educate

  (incorrect information; threats);
- the standard letter from your LEA to home educators asks for timetables, qualifications of tutors, and a description of the room in which education will take place

  (unreasonable demands - these are not legal requirements);
- the LEA inspector made no attempt to establish a friendly relationship with your child; he was abrupt and domineering, and your child was therefore unable to demonstrate her level of understanding in conversation with him

  (rudeness);
- he made it plain that he believed that school was the proper place for all children

  (prejudice);

- he told you that your proposal to home educate was unlikely to be approved because you are not qualified

  (misleading terminology: you are not proposing to educate your child - you are exercising your right to do so; error of fact: there is no legal obligation to be qualified);

- he complained about lack of written work but refused to hear your justification or to let you explain the positive features of your educational programme

  (prejudice);

- he complained that you were not following the national curriculum and would not accept that it does not apply to 'otherwise' education

  (unreasonable demand; false information);

- he refused to listen, his inspection of written work was cursory, and he appeared to have made his mind up before he came

  (bias; unreasonableness);

- he failed to send you a copy of his report when asked

  (not giving reasons for dissatisfaction; and perhaps also not keeping promises).

These are all typical and frequent complaints made of a minority of LEAs. You are unlikely to be subjected to this sort of harassment, but if you are, you should talk to your local coordinator about it first if possible. You may be dealing with an unfortunate individual in an otherwise reasonable LEA. In this case friendly communication may resolve the problem, possibly giving you a better inspector. But where the LEA as a whole are being unreasonable, you may be doing other local members a service by complaining to the local ombudsman.

Your complaint will only be successful if you can show that the maladministration has caused you to suffer actual injustice. If injustice resulting from maladministration is found, the local ombudsman will usually want to suggest to the LEA how it can be remedied. Typical injustice could include:

- fear of prosecution;
- fear of care orders, special boarding schools, etc.;

- fear of a child being forced to return to school;
- anxiety and strain, especially on children (e.g. nightmares and bedwetting which persist until the pressure is removed and then stop);
- unnecessary delay in starting home education, which has since solved all the child's problems.

Often the remedy may simply be a written apology and an undertaking to behave better in future. One thing you can't do is ask for the LEA to pronounce themselves satisfied with your arrangements. They are entitled to make up their own minds about this, so long as they behave reasonably in the course of reaching their decision.

If your complaint is to be effective, you will probably need to send supporting documents with it. This should be no problem if you have kept a file of correspondence with the LEA, including copies of your own letters. If possible, make further copies for the ombudsman, so that you still have a set in case anything goes astray. You may also want to add notes of any phone calls or meetings. (This is one reason why it's a good idea to have someone with you when you have an appointment with an LEA officer. Not only can they give you moral support, but they may also be useful as a witness.) Finally, don't forget to keep a copy of your complaint for reference.

Most complaints received by the ombudsman do not result in a formal report, but this does not mean that complaining is a waste of time. Once the ombudsman is involved, the problem can often be resolved surprisingly quickly to the satisfaction of both parties.

Some solicitors discourage recourse to the ombudsman and are scathing about him 'having no teeth'. On the other hand, the ombudsman is often better informed than most solicitors about the legal aspects of home education, and has a reputation for intelligent and fair reports, cutting through the bureaucracy with a common sense which is perhaps not available to the legal system. Local councils are almost invariably very keen to avoid being the subject of adverse reports from the local ombudsman. It would be unusual if an LEA failed to respect the ombudsman's decision. And you can never be worse off as a result of making a complaint.

Some things the local ombudsman can't do

- The local ombudsman has no power to investigate matters internal to schools and colleges. For instance, you can't complain that your child has been unfairly treated in school.
- The local ombudsman can't investigate your complaint if you have already gone to court or appealed to the Secretary of State.
- Unless there are good reasons for the delay, the local ombudsman can't investigate something you knew about more than a year before complaining. (But of course there's no reason why you shouldn't include things that happened more than a year ago in your evidence if they are relevant to something that has happened since.)

Other ombudsmen

If your complaint is about a government department (such as a complaint about the DSS over child benefit), you should ask your MP to approach the parliamentary ombudsman on your behalf. Complaints about the NHS can be made to the health service ombudsman direct. (See page 126 for addresses.)

3.13 Getting legal advice

Finding a solicitor

No solicitor is an expert in the law relating to 'otherwise' education. On the other hand, few home educators know as much as the average solicitor about the way the legal system works. So if you are involved in a conflict where legal action is a possibility, it may be advisable to look for a solicitor.

The ideal solicitor is radical, interested in human rights issues, and possibly experienced in child care and/or women's refuge cases - all-women practices have proved very supportive to EO. They should be willing to make use of expertise within EO and work as equals with experienced non-professionals. Families have had time and money wasted by solicitors who are too protective of their professional status, who try to research everything from scratch, and who make mistakes because they are unaware of how the theory works out in practice. (Very few home education cases ever get to court.)

The best way to find a sympathetic solicitor is on personal recommendation. Another possibility is to ask Liberty (the National Council for Civil Liberties - see page 126) if they have a solicitor member in your area. Legal advice can turn out to be very expensive unless you qualify for legal aid (see page 120), and not all solicitors do legal aid work; so this may be a point to take into account when trying to find one. You can get the names of legal aid solicitors from citizens' advice bureaux, law centres or the Legal Aid office (see page 126), and they are also identified by the legal aid logo in *Yellow pages*. Citizens' advice bureaux often keep lists of solicitors who are members of Liberty too; or they may be able to give you the address of the local Liberty secretary.

Citizens' advice bureaux and public libraries should hold the *Solicitors' regional directory*. This publication identifies solicitors who are members of the legal aid and fixed fee (see page 121) schemes. It also indicates which areas of the law particular firms specialise in, but the information is supplied by the firms themselves and should be treated with caution. The Law Society produces more specialised lists than this, including one of the panel of solicitors to represent children and other parties in proceedings under the Children Act 1989. This provides a good indication of a general interest in child and family law, but of course it doesn't guarantee any specific knowledge of the law of education.

Some solicitors may work regularly for the local authority you are in conflict with. Perhaps this shouldn't matter, but it does. For this reason it may be best to avoid local solicitors unless you can be sure of their impartiality. EO members have distressing accounts of being misled and let down in these circumstances:

> ▸ It was quite a straightforward case, and at first he was wholehearted in his support. Then he suddenly changed and said I couldn't possibly win. He tried to get me just to send the girls to school so as to avoid court. I said there was no way I would give in when they were doing so much better at home. I went through it all again and thought I'd convinced him, but he let me down badly in court. I found out later that he was friendly with Mr W-- and they played golf together. I handled the appeal myself and won on a point of law, because the first hearing was such a shambles.

In another case a mother sent her son to live with his grandmother during the week in order to put him out of reach of his old school. She and her sister had read up the law and worked out this solution on their own, before they knew of EO. The ESWs were furious at this evasion and harassed them viciously. They were determined not to let them win in court. A local coordinator was present at an interview with the solicitor, and later reported:

> ▸ The solicitor waited until I'd left and then saw her again. She told her that the LEA solicitor had given her a message, but this wasn't blackmail or plea bargaining; if she pleaded guilty they wouldn't tell the DSS that she had falsely claimed social security for her son while he was living with his grandmother. She went on to assure her that she wouldn't get a heavy fine because she had her son's interests at heart.

This threat finished the mother, as it was meant to do. She already felt near to breakdown and had a younger child who was ill. She hadn't made a false statement as such, but it hadn't occurred to her to tell the DSS that her circumstances had changed, since in any case the money had been going to the grandmother to feed the boy. She gave up and pleaded guilty, although she was not. The LEA took no further steps: they only wanted to be vindicated in court.

The family later made enquiries and found that the bulk of their solicitor's work came from the council. The mother had no witnesses and nothing in writing, so she had no evidence of professional misconduct and could not make an official complaint. In this situation, as in interviews with LEA officers, she would have been well advised to take notes of the solicitor's advice, read them back, and ask her to confirm them.

Legal aid

This section describes the legal aid scheme in England and Wales. There are similar schemes for Scotland and Northern Ireland, but you should enquire locally for details.

When applying for legal aid you should be able to give details and produce evidence of your income, savings and commitments. If you are on income support you only need your reference number and the name of the office which pays it. If you qualify for legal aid you may be able to get free legal advice, or, depending on your means, you may be asked to make a contribution.

You can get initial advice and assistance from a solicitor under the **green form scheme**. This normally covers up to two hours' worth of work, but this could sometimes be all you need even if you have to go to court. If you qualify on financial grounds, you can get green form aid immediately and automatically. Most citizens' advice bureaux can advise you on your entitlement, or you can apply directly to any solicitor in the scheme. You can't normally get green form legal aid twice from different solicitors on the same matter.

Whatever your income, you can also often get free advice and representation from the **duty solicitor** on your first appearance at a magistrates' court. However, this is not likely to be a good idea, particularly where home education is concerned. It's better to apply for legal aid beforehand so your solicitor can prepare your case.

If you are charged with an offence you can also apply to the court for **criminal legal aid**. This covers the cost of a solicitor to prepare your defence and to represent you in court. It can also cover the cost of a barrister if you need one, and advice in connection with any appeal.

Applying for criminal legal aid is more complicated. You can apply yourself, but it's generally best to get a solicitor to do it for you. There will be a charge, but if you're already on green form aid it can come out of that. The court must decide that it is in the 'interests of justice' for you to be represented, and that you need help with costs.

You will probably have to wait about six weeks for a decision on criminal legal aid. If you fail to get it the court will write and tell you why. If your first application is unsuccessful you can apply again at any stage. Unless you are on income support you may be asked to pay a contribution, but if you are acquitted this is likely to be returned.

This is only a short summary. The Legal Aid office (see page 126) publishes leaflets containing more detailed information, including 'A practical guide to legal aid' and 'What to do if you get a summons or are questioned by the police'.

Fixed fee interview

In addition to the legal aid schemes, you can get an initial interview of up to half an hour with some solicitors under the £5 fixed fee interview scheme. This applies regardless of whether you qualify for legal aid. In the course of the interview you can find out if you qualify for legal aid.

Talking to your solicitor

Don't forget your solicitor's time costs money, and do your best to avoid wasting it. Even if you're on legal aid, you'll only have a limited time allocation, so you may need to be careful not to exceed it. Have all the necessary information to hand, and take all the relevant letters and documents. (It would be wise to make copies of them first if you possibly can.) And make a note beforehand of any questions you know you will want to ask.

Ask not what EO can do for you...

Education Otherwise is about self-help. If you are starting out on home-based education we hope that by joining the Association you will benefit from the support of other members.

People who get such support often say, 'How can I ever thank you?'

The answer is always essentially the same: pass the gift on to others.

Take courage as you realise your own abilities. Let that confidence flow into all areas of your life. Soon you may get the chance to support another family in turn.

The best way to support a family is not by doing everything *for* them, but by *empowering* them, as you were empowered, to find and develop their own strengths, and to do the job for themselves.

4.1 Education Otherwise

Education Otherwise is a self-help organisation for families practising or contemplating home-based education. It takes its name from section 36 of the Education Act 1944, which gives parents responsibility for their children's education 'either by regular attendance at school or otherwise'.

EO aims to uphold the right of all families to take back direct responsibility for their children's education instead of delegating it to schools. It pursues this aim largely by facilitating mutual support and the exchange of information and experience. EO does not condone disrespect for the law; nor does it deliberately seek confrontation with the authorities. It believes that parents and the state have a common interest in the well-being of children, and should further it by working in partnership.

EO is not committed to any 'correct' system of education, and it does not undertake to provide syllabuses or materials. Rather it tries to help families establish what is suited to the needs of their own children, in accordance with their own beliefs. EO takes the view that children's wishes and feelings should be respected, and that they should play as large a part as practicable in making decisions about their own education. None of this implies that children should be separated from society at large. 'Otherwise' education should allow children to achieve their potential and to play a full part in society.

Education Otherwise was formed by a small group of parents around the beginning of 1977. Since then it has grown steadily, adopting the legal status of a company limited by guarantee. EO now has well over 2000 subscribers distributed widely throughout the UK and beyond. However much their views and motivations may differ, they all share a basic interest in education otherwise than at school.

EO is not a centralised organisation and has no permanent staff or paid workers. Its funding comes from subscriptions and donations, and in order to function it depends on the work, commitment and participation of its members. EO has a network of over 70 voluntary local coordinators spread over the country, who are usually willing to give personal support to members in their area. They are backed up by a number of people with more specialised experience in various aspects of 'otherwise' education.

EO's main decision-making meetings are held three times a year in different parts of the country, usually in conjunction with a more general gathering where members can meet informally. These meetings are traditionally open, and all members are welcome to attend them, whether as observers or participants. Other events are held from time to time, both nationally and locally. In the past these have included workshops for children, camping weeks, residential weekends, conferences/seminars on different aspects of 'otherwise' education, and public meetings. Local groups are active in many areas and often organise their own meetings, visits and activities.

EO publishes a national **newsletter** every two months, and a **contact list**, generally about once a year. Some local groups publish their own newsletters as well. A number of **other publications** are also available from EO, usually with discounts to new and existing members, and a copy of the current list is available on request.

An increasing number of parents and children want an alternative to school. As interest in home-based education spreads, the association continues to grow. The larger the membership, the more clearly EO's voice can be heard.

Education Otherwise
PO Box 7420, London N9 9SG

For recorded list of contacts, phone 0891 518303

(Calls cost 39p per minute evenings and weekends, 49p per minute daytime, and should last no longer than about 3 minutes. Income raised from phone calls helps to support EO.)

4.2 Other organisations

Advisory Centre for Education (ACE)

1b Aberdeen Studios,
22 Highbury Grove, London
N5 2EA; tel. 0171-354 8321
(Monday-Friday, 2.00-5.00).

Publishes *ACE bulletin,* and a range of booklets and information sheets on various aspects of education in Britain. Publications list available.

Anti Bullying Campaign

10 Borough High Street, London
SE1 9QQ; tel. 0171-378 1446
(Monday-Friday, 10.00-5.00).

Children's Legal Centre

University of Essex,
Wivenhoe Park, Colchester,
Essex CO4 3SQ;
tel. 01206 873820

Advice and information on law and policy affecting children and young people in England and Wales. Monthly bulletin *Childright.*

Correspondence colleges

Association of British Correspondence Colleges

6 Francis Grove, London
SW19 4DT; tel. 0181-544 9559.

Publishes a free list of member colleges and their courses.

World-Wide Education Service of the PNEU

St George's House,
14-17 Wells Street, London
W1P 3FP; tel. 0171-637 2644

Primary level.

Mercers College

Ware, Herts SG12 9BU;
tel. (01920) 465926.

Age 13-15.

National Extension College

18 Brooklands Avenue,
Cambridge CB2 2HN;
tel. (01223) 316644.

Education Now

P.O. Box 186, Ticknall, Derbys
DE7 1WF.

Publish alternative education booklets (mostly *not* about home education), plus the magazine *Education now.*

Kidscape

152 Buckingham Palace Road,
London SW1W 9TR;
tel. 0171-730 3300.

Campaign for children's safety from bullying and abuse.

Law Centres Federation

18-19 Warren Street, London
W1P 5DB; tel. 0171-387 8570.

Legal Aid

England & Wales

Legal Aid Head Office,
29-37 Red Lion Street, London
WC1R 4PP; tel. 0171-813 5300.

Northern Ireland

Incorporated Law Society of
Northern Ireland,
Legal Aid Department,
Bedford House,
16-22 Bedford Street, Belfast
BT2 7FL; tel. (01232) 246441.

Scotland

Scottish Legal Aid Board,
44 Drumsheugh Gardens,
Edinburgh EH3 7SW;
tel. 0131-226 7061.

Liberty (National Council for Civil Liberties)

21 Tabard Street, London
SE1 4LA; tel. 0171-403 3888.

National Association for Gifted Children

Park Campus,
Boughton Green Road,
Northampton NN2 7AL;
tel. 01604 792300.
(Moving to Milton Keynes)

National Council for Vocational Qualifications

222 Euston Road, London
NW1 2BZ; tel. 0171-387 9898.

Ombudsmen

Local Government:
England

21 Queen Anne's Gate, London
SW1H 9BU; tel. 0171-915 3210.

Beverley House,
17 Shipton Road, York
YO3 6FZ; tel. (01904) 663200.

There are three local ombudsmen for England: the one for the North of England and the North Midlands is based at York, and the other two are based in London.

Northern Ireland

33 Wellington Place, Belfast
BT1 6HN; tel. (01232) 233821.

Scotland

23 Walker Street, Edinburgh
EH3 7HX; tel. 0131-225 5300.

Wales

Derwen House, Court Road,
Bridgend, Mid-Glamorgan
CF31 1BN; tel. (01656) 661325.

You can get a leaflet from one of these addresses explaining how to make a complaint. In the case of the ombudsmen for England and Northern Ireland, the information is contained in a booklet which also includes a complaint form.

Parliamentary ombudsman

Church House,
Great Smith Street,
London SW1P 3BW;
tel. 0171-276 2130/3000.

General enquiries. To complain about a government department, first contact your MP.

Health service ombudsman: England

Millbank Tower, Millbank,
London SW1P 4QP;
tel. 0171-276 2035.

Scotland

1 Atholl Place, Edinburgh
EH3 8HP; tel. 0131-225 7465.

Wales

Fourth floor,
Pearl Assurance House,
Greyfriars Road, Cardiff
CF1 3AG; tel. 0222 394621.

Enquiries and complaints.

Open School

Park Road, Dartington, Totnes,
Devon TQ9 6EQ;
tel. (01803) 866542; fax 866676.

Distance learning based on national curriculum materials for people without other access to specialist tuition. Includes 'tutafax' - learning by fax.

PAIN: Parents Against Injustice

10 Water Lane,
Bishop's Stortford, Herts
CM23 2JZ; tel. 01279 656564.

'Advice and support for those who state they have been mistakenly involved in investigations of alleged child abuse'

Scottish Child Law Centre

Cranston House,
108 Argyle Street, Glasgow
G2 8BH; tel. 0141-226 3737
(Tuesday-Friday, 10.00-4.00).

Scottish Council for Civil Liberties (SCCL)

146 Holland Street, Glasgow
G2 4NG; tel. 0141-332 5960
(Monday-Friday, 2.00-5.00).

Special needs

AFASIC: Association For All Speech-Impaired Children

347 Central Market, Smithfield,
London EC1A 9NH;
tel. 0171-236 6487.

British Dyslexia Association

98 London Road, Reading, Berks
RG1 5AU; tel. 01734 668271.

Myalgic Encephalomyelitis (ME) Association

Stanhope House, High Street, Stanford-Le-Hope, Essex SS7 0HA; tel. 01375 642466.

Costs for programmes provided by the following organisations can be quite high, but trust funding may be obtainable:

BIRD Centre (Brain Injury Rehabilitation and Development)

131 Main Road, Broughton, Chester CH4 0NR; tel. (01244) 532047 (9.30-10.00 a.m.)

Brainwave Centre for Rehabilitation and Development

Marsh Lane, Huntworth Gate, Bridgwater, Somerset TA6 6LQ; tel. (01278) 429089.

Individually tailored programmes of developmental education. Family orientated approach, with children seen as an opportunity rather than a problem.

British Institute for Brain Injured Children

Knowle Hall, Bridgwater, Somerset TA7 8PJ; tel. (01278) 684060.

For all kinds of special needs. Teaches parents programmes of stimulation therapy to be carried out at home.

Option Institute and Fellowship

R.D. #1, Box 174a, Sheffield, Mass. 01257, USA; tel. 413-229-2100, 229-8062.

'Happiness is a choice': home-based, child-centred, parent-directed alternative for parents and interested professionals.

Contact a Family

170 Tottenham Court Road, London W1P 0HA; tel. 0171-383 3555.

Contact address for other organisations concerned with special needs at both national and local level.

INDEX